YOU'RE IN CONTROL

Planning the Most Important Retirement in the World – *Yours*

Financial Thought-Leaders Series

USA Financial Media

Printed in Grand Rapids, Michigan

Graphic designer: Lee May
Copy editor: Christine Steele

Published by USA Financial Media
6020 E. Fulton St., Ada, Michigan, 49301

ISBN-10: 0-9984010-0-5
ISBN-13: 978-0-9984010-0-3

Printed in the United States of America

Every effort was made to provide the most current, correct, and clearly expressed information possible. However, inadvertent errors can occur, and tax rules and regulations often change.

The information in this book is not intended to serve as legal, tax, or accounting advice, and readers are encouraged to seek guidance from a financial professional. The authors and publisher disclaim any responsibility for any misunderstanding on the part of the readers and in any individual situation or position taken by a taxpayer.

IMPORTANT DISCLOSURES

The content discussed is strictly educational in nature and is not intended as personal financial advice.

You should seek the help of a qualified financial professional regarding any strategies discussed as everyone's situation is unique.

Examples provided in this book are for illustrative purposes only and are not representative of specific products, strategies, rates, or accounts. All rates mentioned are hypothetical and for example purposes only.

No investment strategy can guarantee a profit or prevent against a loss. Investing carries an inherent element of risk, including the potential for loss of principal and income.

Plan First, Invest Second and Asset Cycle Portfolio System are registered trademarks of USA Financial Plug-N-Run.

For specific tax- or estate-planning advice, please consult a qualified tax advisor or estate-planning attorney. The authors contributing to the content of this book are not attorneys. The content provided herein is not intended as legal or tax advice.

Indexes mentioned are provided as benchmarks and are not available vehicles for investment. You cannot invest directly in an index.

The contents of this book are not endorsed by or affiliated with the Social Security Administration, or any other government agency.

Examples containing insurance products are for illustrative purposes only and may not be available to all readers. Insurance products, such as life insurance, often require an applicant to qualify through an underwriting process. Additional costs for various features and riders on these types of products may apply.

Annuities are best suited for long-term investors. Withdrawals from an annuity prior to age 59½ may be subject to an additional 10% tax penalty. Guarantees on an annuity are provided by the claims-paying ability of the underlying insurance company. Surrender schedules may apply.

CONTENTS

FOREWORD

As a part of the Financial Thought-Leaders Series, *You're in Control* seeks to share with readers a different perspective on retirement planning. Each chapter is personally written by individuals who make their profession in financial coaching, investment management and retirement planning. Their goal is to help get you to and through retirement with greater confidence.

The authors of this book come from a variety of educational, professional, and geographical backgrounds — yet they share one thing in common — every day they help people like you. Collectively, they've helped to plan the retirement of thousands of Americans throughout the country.

Whether you choose to DIY or seek the advice of a financial professional, the confidence that can come from the development and implementation of a financial plan cannot be understated. And the only way not to read this book is with a closed mind, because a closed mind isn't capable of appreciating a new perspective.

All the best,
Mark R. Mersman
Co-host of the nationally syndicated USA Financial Radio Show
Co-contributor of the audiobook, *The Retiree's Guide to Retirement Income Planning*
Grand Rapids, Michigan

Mark Mersman is an investment advisor representative of, and securities are offered through, USA Financial Securities, 6020 E. Fulton St., Ada, MI 49301. Member FINRA/SIPC (finra.org) and a registered investment advisor.

INTRODUCTION

On December 31, 1999, many Americans waited anxiously for the clock to strike midnight. It was a New Year's Eve unlike any other. The hype surrounding that particular New Year's Eve was unmatched, with media outlets worldwide stirring the pot and striking fear and panic in the hearts of many. It was dubbed "Y2K," and as you'll recall, when computers around the globe "rolled" into the new millennia, it was feared it could incite pandemonium and wreak havoc on our lives in immeasurable ways.

Pundits predicted a range of potential possibilities for what might happen. Our computerized world would come to a screeching halt because we only accounted for years in two digits. The year 2000 would throw a nasty curveball to computers across the globe making them think it was the year 1900. Power grids would shut down. Our banking systems would go haywire. Anything that was reliant on computers was at great risk for failure.

As a result, many people fled to their local grocery and hardware stores, stocking up on everything from canned goods and water to guns and generators. Many Americans went so far as to build underground bunkers to flee to for safety in the event of total chaos in the streets. Would there be looting? Would the hooligans seize the opportunity for chaos? Would the world end? What would happen?

As the clock neared midnight, people braced themselves for the worst. And, as the clock struck midnight, many were shocked by what had happened.

NOTHING.

No power outages. No looting. Our financial system didn't come crashing down. Outside of a few inconveniences for computer technicians, Y2K (or the millennium bug) was nothing more than a media storm.

Or was it?

Is it possible that the year 2000 brought about a change that was much more subtle? A change that wasn't truly noticed until many years later?

If you look closely at a chart of the stock market, you'll notice something rather drastic took place in the year 2000. It marked the end of a bull run that lasted nearly two decades. In fact, from 1982–2000, the Dow Jones Industrial Average rose a cumulative 1,408% over a 17.5-year period. What's amazing about that statistic is that it included Black Monday. You may recall Monday, October 19, 1987, when stock markets around the world crashed. The Dow Jones Industrial Index dropped by 508 points to 1738.74 (a loss of 22.61%). Despite that record-breaking, single-day drop, the DJIA finished positive for the entire year of 1987.

The 20 years prior to Y2K were an era marked by some interesting trends. The growth of the mutual fund industry was astonishing. Much of this growth could be attributed to the widespread adoption of 401(k) plans by employers. Many companies chose to shift from traditional defined benefit pensions to defined contribution plans like the 401(k). In fact, according to the Center for Retirement Research, in 1980 more than 60% of private sector workers were covered by a defined benefit pension plan. By the year 2000, less than 15% of private sector workers were covered. The reason? The 401(k) allowed companies to shift the retirement responsibility from them to YOU, the average American worker.

The truth is, most people didn't mind when this was happening — either that, or they didn't really understand the magnitude of what was happening. With the success of the stock market at the time, most Americans didn't mind investing for their future because the bull market worked in their favor. Plus, 401(k)s gave the average American something they had never had before with their retirement — CONTROL. We could control where we invested, as well as when and how much we took out.

Y2K

I'm not saying that the computer challenges of Y2K are to blame for this "shift" we are discussing. It's purely coincidental, but, nonetheless, a fascinating correlation.

On January 1, 2000, the Dow Jones Industrial Average was hovering around 11,500. A decade later, as the stock markets closed on December 31, 2009, that same index was at 10,428. It's not-so-affectionately known as "the lost decade," because investors essentially lost a decade's worth of time for the growth of their assets.

The 2000s were marked by two devastatingly painful market downturns — the tech bubble of the early 2000s and the credit crisis or financial crisis of 2008–09. I'm not sharing anything new with you when I remind you of these two stretches of time. I must ask though — what did you do with your investments during that time? Did you enjoy the "control" you had over your portfolio during the lost decade? Do you remember how you felt in late 2008?

It didn't really matter how old you were at the time — it was scary. Jobs were being lost at record levels. Portfolios were beat up, and the retirement dreams of many were altered with each passing day. When I think of that period, there are two quotes that come to mind by two people who rose to fame (and infamy) in quite different ways.

The first quote is by the famed investor Warren Buffett. He once quipped, "Only when the tide goes out do you discover who's been swimming naked." In the 2000s, the tide went out twice, and many people were exposed (financially speaking, of course). People began to realize they may have been taking more risk in their portfolios than they could truly handle. The way I see it, one of the biggest lessons to learn from that time frame was to respect risk. Unfortunately, as 2008–09 gets further away from us in our rearview mirror, we tend to respect risk less and less.

The second quote is from professional boxer Mike Tyson. Tyson once said, "Everyone has a plan till they get punched in the mouth." Obviously, he was referring to his bouts in the boxing ring, but the quote holds quite true for those of us who have an investment portfolio. The question to ask yourself is this: Could your financial plan withstand a punch in the mouth? I'm not talking about only your investments. You must understand that having investments and pie charts is NOT a financial plan. A comprehensive plan is about much more than a "bagful of investments." It incorporates everything from retirement income planning (Social Security, pension, investments) to insurance and wealth transfer.

Comprehensive financial planning addresses the "what-ifs" that are lingering out there. Those what-ifs are the potential punches in the mouth. What if you needed long-term health care tomorrow? What if your spouse died tomorrow? What if tax rates go up? What if the stock market goes down? What if you live to be 105?

There are thousands of financial professionals out there that can help you fill your bag full of investments. In fact, today you can do that online, with a few clicks of a mouse. However, you must not forget that a bagful of investments is NOT a financial plan. This book was written by advisors who believe that planning first and investing second is a must. They've been individually selected to share ideas and concepts with you that will help you navigate retirement and financial planning in the 21st century.

Retiring in the 21st century is unlike any other time in history. Our retirement will be vastly different than the retirement of our parents and grandparents. We're living longer. The stock market has changed forever. Tax laws are becoming more and more complex. There are medical and technological advances taking place every day.

We have control. That can be a good thing or a bad thing. It's a good thing if you empower yourself with knowledge and seek the guidance and direction of professionals who can help you reach your goals. Control is a bad thing if you shut down the roadway to information and knowledge. This book will open your mind to new ideas and concepts that may benefit your financial situation. The authors work with people like you every day and have helped them navigate the shift from their working life to life after work. They have engineered the retirements of hundreds and hundreds of Americans. I'm confident when I say that their insights may help engineer the most important retirement in the world … YOURS.

It's your retirement. It's your life. You have the control.

Chapter 1

The Great American Retirement Crisis

By Andrew J. Paladino, CPA, MSF

The meaning of *retirement* is and has been changing for several years now. Americans are realizing that what retirement meant is just that. It means something else. One would work and be loyal to one company for years, and at the end of those years the company would take care of them financially until the employee, and if a spouse, passed away. In addition, there would be Social Security benefits provided by the U.S. government. However, times are changing, resulting in the impending retirement crisis. Or, perhaps, the crisis is not impending — it is here now. It is our wakeup call. We are responsible for our own retirement.

Meet My Father

My father was a hard and devoted worker and remained loyal to the same company for 35 years. He moved up the ranks, eventually becoming a top executive. While we grew up in a modest Midwestern home, we were never denied anything. He provided for my mother, sister and me. I was just starting my career out of college, working for a large local CPA firm when my father decided to take an early retirement. I am sure my parents discussed and evaluated their options. He would receive a monthly pension payment close to his normal salary. Coupled with the Social Security payments, this would be my parents' retirement income. I remember my dad eventually taking on part-time jobs, either because he wanted to find something to do or to provide extra income. I imagine it was more of the former, as he enjoyed stints coaching high school sports teams and driving a school bus. After my dad's passing, my mother continued to receive the income.

Work is different now. Less and less are working for just one company. In fact, if you have worked for only one company during your career and look to make a change, you may be asked why you have not made changes in the past. Job security is also no longer a promise, and pensions and the pension system could be coming to an end. Add in the problems looming for Social Security and Medicare, in combination with the growing U.S. deficit and debt. We must come to the realization that we need to think and act differently about our future.

Why is this happening? Let us look at all of it and what is in store for the future.

Do You Have a Pension? If So, Will You Actually Get It?

The two issues with pension plans are whether or not you actually have one, and if so, is it properly funded. The three components funding retirement are typically Social Security, pensions, and your own money. The pension piece would be provided by your employer. The employer establishes a retirement plan and funds it to meet the projected payments made in the future to their retired workforce and spouses. However, the number of companies that have pension plans in place is declining. Others have decided to either freeze their plans or terminate them by offering distributions to the participants.

According to the U.S. Bureau of Labor Statistics, less than 20% of employees are covered by pensions, down approximately one half from just 15 years ago.[1] Typically, larger companies are the most likely to have pension plans in place for their employees. The trend for many years now, though, has been to replace the traditional pension plan with an employee-driven plan, the familiar 401(k). If you look at the history of 401(k) plans, they were originally introduced as an additional option for an employee to save for retirement. Many employers eventually navigated away from their pension plans and their increasing funding costs, instead offering to contribute or match money into the 401(k) plan. I believe many employees at the time thought this was of great benefit to them, not understanding the eventual dwindling of their employer-provided pension benefit. The trend toward abandoning pension plans in favor of 401(k)s continued and increased over the past few decades. So in all likelihood, you do not have the pension portion of your retirement funding.

However, there are many people who still have access to a pension plan. Projections are that approximately $3 trillion is in these plans.[2] Sounds like a lot, but is it really? It is, but it is not enough. Many of the plans are underfunded. The percentage of employers with fully funded pension plans declined from 84% in 1998 to 37% in 2002, according to a study by the international consulting firm Willis Towers Watson. The market value of unfunded liabilities was $3.28 trillion in 2013.[3] All of this can be traced back to stock market losses over the past 15 years (think 2001 and 2008), lowering interest rates, questionable accounting practices, and senior executives who have taken care of their own retirement through golden parachutes, having no issues with positioning pension liabilities to be shed through bankruptcy, mergers, or conversion of plans. Some have termed this "The Great American Pension-Fund Robbery."

In 1974, the Employee Retirement Income Security Act (ERISA) classified underfunding of pension plans. If the value of their assets fell below 90% of their current liabilities, the plans had five years to resolve the deficit and be fully funded. In June 2015, the Internal Revenue Service issued procedures and regulations explaining how a pension plan in critical and declining status can apply for approval to suspend benefits. This affects those currently retired and receiving benefits and those counting on their benefits for the future.

According to a study by the Center for Retirement Research at Boston College, if you are in or have access to an "old school" pension plan, then you should have concerns. Under federal law, you must be informed if your plan is seriously underfunded. The government provides three warning labels to underfunded plans: endangered, severely endangered, and critical. The Department of Labor provides a list of these plans on its website.[4]

In addition, an article by the U.S. Social Security Administration, Office of Retirement and Disability Policy titled "The Disappearing Defined Benefit Pension and Its Potential Impact on the Retirement Incomes of Baby Boomers" summarizes its findings:

This article uses a microsimulation model to estimate how freezing all remaining private-sector and one-third of all public-sector defined benefit (DB) pension plans over the next 5 years would affect retirement incomes of baby boomers. If frozen plans were supplemented with new or enhanced defined contribution (DC) retirement plans, there would be more losers than winners, and average family incomes would decline. The decline in family income would be much larger for last-wave boomers born from 1961 through 1965 than for those born from 1946 through 1950, because younger boomers are more likely to have their DB pensions frozen with relatively little job tenure. Higher DC accruals would raise retirement incomes for some families by more than their lost DB benefits. But about 26 percent of last-wave boomers would have lower family incomes at age 67, and only 11 percent would see their income increase.[5]

There are also major concerns and issues when we look at pensions in the public sector (state and local governments). I have met several people who had maintained their state government job because at retirement they were promised a beneficial pension. Are these pensions strong now? Consider these factors:

- As of 2014, public sector pension in total were underfunded by $4.7 trillion, up from $4.1 trillion in 2013.[6]
- The state of Illinois's pension plans is only about 40% funded. Eight other states are less than 60% funded (Alaska, Connecticut, Hawaii, Kansas, Kentucky, Louisiana, New Hampshire, and Rhode Island).[7] Many other states are also having funding issues.
- Some public service employees do not participate in Social Security

and rely on their government pension as the primary source of retirement income.

- In 2015, New Jersey had a $1.57 billion pension budget gap that the state is not required to fill, according to a New Jersey Supreme Court ruling.[8]

What does this all mean? If you have a pension plan paying you now or in the future, should you be concerned? You bet. Is it not, though, guaranteed by the government? Many people I meet with who have pensions tell me there is no need to worry. Correct? Well, maybe yes, maybe no.

The guarantee they are referring to is the coverage by the U.S. government through the Pension Benefit Guaranty Corporation (PBGC). The PBGC is a quasi-government agency established in September 1974 by former president Gerald Ford. It was set up to protect the pension payments of workers who face the possibility of reduced or no retirement security. Its goals are to:

- Preserve plans and protect pensioners;
- Pay pension benefits on time and accurately; and
- Maintain high standards of stewardship and accountability.

Meet Frank

I met Frank and his wife after they both had retired. They were living on Frank's pension from a large steel company where he worked all of his life and from where he retired. They also had Social Security income. They had saved some money and wanted ideas for protecting their savings and earning money on it. Frank received a monthly pension check from his employer's pension plan. Several years later, the steel company was having some financial difficulties, but Frank's fellow retired workers said he should not be concerned because his pension was guaranteed by the government. Although Frank's check was still sent to him, he learned it was going to come from the Pension Benefit

Guaranty Corporation and would be three-quarters of the normal amount of his check. A few years later he received another notice that his monthly check would be one-half of its original amount! They were now looking at the possibility of using their savings for income.

At least Frank received benefits from the PBGC, but there are now concerns about its financial stability. According to PBGC's annual report (fiscal year ending September 30, 2014), the PBGC became responsible for an additional 106 insolvent employer plans covering approximately 57,300 participants. In total, the PBGC now covers 41 million pensioners in over 24,000 plans. Unfortunately, it does not guarantee the entire amount of a worker's pension. Indeed, PBGC's liabilities far exceed its assets. Back in May 2003, PBGC went from a surplus of $7.7 billion to deficit of $5.4 million. As of September 30, 2014, PBGC's financial position decreased by $26.133 million, increasing its deficit from $35.639 million as of September 30, 2013, to $61,772 million.[9] Consider those numbers a bit more. The deficit for that fiscal year went up more than 70% from the prior year!

The pension crisis is indeed upon us. If you currently are receiving a pension, then I advise that you develop a contingency plan in case your payments are reduced. If you are counting on a pension in the future, whether it is five years from now or 15, it would be wise to look for other sources of retirement income.

Social Security Income

Could that other source of income be your Social Security income benefits? Probably/maybe.

Social Security is an important program that provides retirement and disability income to 60 million Americans. It is also the largest federal program, accounting for nearly one-quarter of all federal spending. Despite its dedicated revenues, Social Security promises more benefits in the future than it can deliver. Since 2010, Social Security has been paying out more than it takes in, on an annual basis, and its trustees warn that the program cannot sustain its projected long-run costs. According to data from the trustees and information calculated by FirstBudget.org:[10]

- The combined Social Security trust funds are projected to be depleted in 2033, which would result in a 23% benefit cut. The Social Security Disability Insurance fund is projected to be depleted in late 2016.

- In 1960, there were approximately five workers paying into the system for each Social Security beneficiary. As the baby boom generation retires, today's ratio of nearly three workers for each beneficiary will shrink to roughly two workers per beneficiary by 2030. This means that without placing a larger tax burden on workers or cutting benefits to retirees, the program will incur large deficits.

- Waiting to address Social Security's finances will require larger cuts or tax increases, spreading this larger burden over fewer people, necessitate abrupt and less-targeted changes, and leave workers with less time to plan and adjust.

Meet Ida May Fuller

Ida May Fuller was the first recipient of Social Security. At age 65, on January 31, 1940, she received her first check of $22.54. She lived to age 100, receiving a total of $22,888.92 in benefits. She worked for three years under the Social Security program. Her accumulated taxes on her salary during those three years was a total of $24.75.[11]

Will Social Security Be There When You Need It?

There is concern that Social Security will be bankrupt in the future, if not sooner. A survey found that about one-quarter of Americans are expecting to receive no Social Security benefits.[12] What is causing this to happen? Consider these three colliding factors:

- Pay-as-you-go financing. Benefits are currently not being paid from savings. Rather, the funding is coming from taxes imposed on younger workers to support those retired.
- Changes in demographics. The ratio of workers paying taxes to those receiving benefits is declining. Factor in that people are living longer.
- The change in the benefit formula. The new formula that sets initial benefits is set to grow faster than inflation.

So what does this mean for our benefits?

The outlook is not good. However, it is not all doom and gloom. In all likelihood, Social Security will not cease to exist. It probably will still be around, but perhaps in a different format or different kind of program. Even if there are only enough reserves to pay 77% of benefits in 2030, politicians are unlikely to slash retirees' benefits.[13] Perhaps the official full retirement age is eventually pushed back. Social Security's original earliest retirement age was 65. It is now 62. Full retirement age was eventually moved from age 65 to 66 and then to 67. Maybe the age is moved farther out. The other discussion involves taxes. The simple fix is to increase the tax on earnings to fund the program. The tax rate could be increased and/or the cap on earnings that are taxed could be raised or eliminated altogether. There could also be a reduction in how benefits are increased and tying increases to different inflation rate calculators.

Bill and Kathy, the Planners

Bill is 50 years old, married, and has two teenagers. When he and his wife Kathy first met with me, they were concerned they were not on the right track to secure their future. Each had well-paying jobs and was doing their best to save for retirement. There were other pressures too — the household budget, providing for the family and their children. They wanted to project where they would be financially in 15 years. We made conservative assumptions, factored in inflation, and looked to determine what retirement income would be for both through age 100. Both had accumulated enough credits to qualify for Social Security benefits, and we accessed the projections online. However, they were adamant about using slightly lower figures for their Social Security income benefits and also wanted to leave them at an even level, with no increases throughout the years. Crazy? Definitely not.

What If Nothing Is Done?

Bill and Kathy were being proactive in anticipating their future income from Social Security. Thoughts are that something will be done to the system. The question is, when? Lawmakers are aware of the problem. Nothing will get resolved unless they act. It is obvious that the issue needs to be addressed soon. However, no matter what or when the government decides to act, my advice is for you to take control of your own retirement income. Your Social Security benefit maybe should be considered just supplemental income in the future. Save more; save wisely (take advantage of employer matches in 401(k), 403(b) plans, etc.; consider Roth accounts). Or as one might say: Get your retirement away from relying on the White House, and get it to your Own House.

Medicare

Medicare remains a large piece of the federal budget despite recent slowdowns in federal health care spending. Lower growth projections have not tempered the uncertainty about how much of the slowdown is from a potential shift in the health care system. The aging population is the main force in the future of health care spending and the increase in those receiving Medicare and Medicaid benefits.

Health care spending is the largest piece of the federal budget, currently more than $900 million, or over one-quarter, of all government spending. Projections are that over the next eight years the annual federal health care spending will grow by 60%, from $1.1 trillion to $1.9 trillion. Over the next 25 years, federal health care spending is projected to grow from 5% of the economy to 8%, faster than any other government program, mainly due to health care cost inflation and an aging population. Historically, the costs of health care have grown faster than the U.S. economy and projections are for this to continue.[14]

This leads us to a discussion on the U.S. debt and deficit.

The U.S. Budget Deficit and Debt

The numbers thrown around regarding the amount of debt the U.S. has and the growing federal deficit have caused confusion for many. Several numbers are used to describe both. The deficit is the difference between what the government takes in (receipts) and outlays (spending like Social Security and Medicare benefits). When there is a deficit, the government must borrow money to pay the bills. The accumulation of this borrowing results in the U.S. debt. Although deficits have fallen in recent years, the amount of debt has continued to grow and is projected to grow in an unsustainable path.

Here are some facts:[15]

- Federal deficits have been over $1 trillion each year from 2009 to 2011. They have come down but are expected to rise again to $489 billion in 2018, $763 billion in 2021, and back to over $1 trillion in 2025.
- Total U.S. debt today is approximately $13 trillion. This represents 74% of the U.S. economy. That equals $105,000 per American family.
- With a continuous growing economy, projections for the next eight years are for the debt to exceed $21 trillion.

Let's stop for a second and try to comprehend what these numbers mean. Perhaps you have read examples of what $1 trillion looks like. Suppose I give you $10,000. Sounds good, right? If I gave it to you in $100 bills, the stack of bills would be about a half-inch high. If I gave the same amount to 99 other people, the stack would be approximately 5 feet tall. But this is $10,000 times 100 people. One trillion is 100 million $10,000s. How tall would that stack be? Almost 800 miles. That is about 144 Mount Everests!

So what does this all mean?

1) A high U.S. debt leads to increased government borrowing. That borrowing hurts other productive investments in the economy and people.
2) Rising debt can lead to higher interest rates. This affects consumer borrowing rates. It also results in an increasing share of the budget to pay for the interest on the debt instead of to the economy and people.
3) Interest payments on the debt are projected to become the fastest growing category of federal spending. There will be approximately $331 billion in interest payments in 2017. In about 10 years, interest payments will reach approximately $800 billion.[16]
4) Projections are that by 2030, 100% of the government's revenue will go toward interest payments and other mandatory spending programs.[17]

Combating waste, fraud, and abuse or even eliminating them would only slightly reduce the deficit. In addition, economic growth is crucial, but alone it will not solve the debt problem. Many programs such as health care programs grow faster when the economy does well, which is counteractive to reducing the deficit. As far as raising income taxes to help solve the problem, estimates are that if taxes were increased on just those making over $250,000, the top rate would have to be over 100%.

This is all a result in a mismatch between the government's revenue and the expenses it pays for what many see are on autopilot. Think Social Security and Medicare. An aging population and one that is living longer will only make this deficit and debt whirlwind continue to spin out of control. The times are definitely changing!

The Winds Have Changed

The meaning of *retirement* is changing. The three-legged stool is a bit wobbly. Pensions are in danger, whether you have one or are expecting one in the future. Your Social Security benefits will probably be available, but perhaps a different amount or you will receive them later than you would like. The pressure that Social Security and other entitlements, such as Medicare, are putting on the U.S. deficit (and eventually increasing the debt) will have to be resolved. Many may have *retirement expectations*, but what is needed is a *retirement plan*. The time has come to recognize that this is not *your parents' retirement.*

The good news is that as you recognize this, you can begin to take control of your own retirement. An abundance of educational materials, programs, tools, techniques, and products are available to help you work toward your retirement future. You will need to understand though, that these are only a part of the plan. The other part is your willingness to embrace the new thinking and new behavior needed for a new era. Retire*ment* is changing to "retire*means*." Full steam ahead! Take control!

Chapter 2

The #1 Enemy to Your Success

By Craig J. Watkins

How many people do you know that you would truly label as "successful?" I don't necessarily mean financially successful, although that certainly counts as one type of success. I'm referring to individuals who are successful in every aspect of their lives. People who enjoy vibrant health, plenty of good friends, are full of energy and curiosity, always learning new things and excited about life. I'm talking about the type of people that you look at and say "they've got it together."

These are the kind of people you enjoy being around because they make you feel at ease. It's likely that these people have enjoyed academic and/or business success. It's not as though these people didn't endure setbacks or face challenges. In fact, it is probably likely that their success is a result of their ability to overcome these challenges.

Perhaps I'm describing you — or perhaps a few of your friends or acquaintances are coming to mind. Have you ever wondered what makes them (or you) successful? What characteristics do they have that others don't?

Would You Fail the Marshmallow Test?

In a 1960s psychological experiment by Stanford University, children were brought into a room one by room. They were asked to sit down. Placed in front of them on a table was one marshmallow. They were told that they could eat it, but if they were able to wait a little while, they could have multiple marshmallows later. The researchers deliberately left the room for 15 minutes. The children were filmed as they squirmed and struggled to delay their desire for instant gratification.

On average, the children held out for no more than a few minutes, although one in three lasted the full 15 minutes and was rewarded with multiple marshmallows.

Years later, the professor in charge of the experiment, Walter Mischel, found that the children who demonstrated an inability to defer gratification were the ones who were more prone to poor academic/scholastic achievement. In addition, they demonstrated a lesser ability to plan and think ahead.

This study has gained an interesting level of attention over the years. In fact, additional studies have been conducted, and it has been surmised that the main difference in the children who could hold out versus those who couldn't resist was not intelligence related but was with self-control. The primary skill of those who delayed gratification (and resisted grabbing the marshmallow) was an ability to distract them (singing songs, twiddling thumbs, etc.).

The primary lesson from Mischel's research is that the number one obstacle to our success is — you guessed it — ourselves. We're our own worst enemy. When it comes to financial matters, self-control is the first discipline we must learn if we wish to enjoy success.

Just Admit It. Age Happens.

There's nothing wrong with being proud of yourself — just don't let it get in the way of your finances. Medicine has come a long way, but (to my knowledge at least) there has not been anything developed to reverse the trend of aging. At some point, we all get older. That some point is today and tomorrow.

You may be surprised to hear that the sweet spot for financial decision-making is at the age of 53[1] – if you're younger than 53, you've got some learning to do yet. If you're over 53, you're on the downward slide. OK, maybe that's being a bit dramatic. However, the research suggests that 53 is our peak age for quality decision-making regarding our finances.

The same research that reported age 53 as our prime decision-making age warned that nearly half of the population who has reached the age of 80 suffers from dementia or other cognitive impairment. Obviously, this compromises ones' ability to make important financial decisions.

For most Americans, they reach the pinnacle of their wealth accumulation as they enter retirement. An interesting connection between this wealth accumulation peak and aging is that quality financial decision-making begins eroding around the same period many have reached the peak of their wealth accumulation. In fact, one study found that financial literacy scores decline by about 1% a year after the age of 60.[2] Interestingly, while half of those in their 80s realize the importance of needing help and obtain it, the other half don't.[3] This presents a large segment of the population that has a dangerous combination of wealth and vulnerability. Scammers and conmen recognize this as well.

It illustrates the importance of having advocates and people looking out for us as we age — these may be professionals, friends, or family.

Critical Decisions

Have you ever been driving down the road and run into a traffic jam? You're not certain the cause of the traffic jam, but your brain goes into overdrive to figure out the quickest way to get from where you are to where you want to go. Do you switch lanes? Do you turn around and find an alternate route? Do you stay in the same lane?

Invariably, whatever decision you make, doesn't it always feel like you made the wrong one? You say to yourself, "I should have switched lanes," or "If I would have taken that side street I could have avoided this."

In our everyday lives, we make these kinds of decisions every day. They are inconsequential in the grand scheme of life. In fact, in many cases, our indecision isn't punished. If I just stay in the same lane, things will work itself out. When it comes to your finances, it's imperative that you recognize that indecision is still a decision. More often than not, it's probably the wrong one.

This is especially true when it comes to investing. Making prudent decisions is the most important job of any investor. A poor investment decision (or indecision) can irreparably harm your long-term success. Unfortunately, our brain is good at tricking us into making poor decisions. Why do we make them? In many cases, they can be traced back to the way the decisions were made — the alternatives were not clearly defined, the right information was not collected, the costs and benefits were not accurately weighed. Oftentimes, the fault lies not just in the decision-making process, but rather **in the mind of the decision-maker**. The way the human brain works can sabotage our decisions.

Anchoring

With most decisions, the mind has a tendency to give a higher level of credence to the first piece of information it receives. It "anchors" itself to this information, well before logic and reason enter the decision-making equation. This is referred to as "anchoring." Just like an anchor on a boat, our mind allows us the freedom to drift a bit, but it doesn't allow us to get too far away from the initial anchor point.

In a moment, we'll share an investing example of anchoring. However, the effects of anchoring are not limited to the world of investing. In fact, anchoring can rear its ugly head with stereotypes, racial or cultural biases, and even everyday business activities.

Many corporations and salespeople will make sales forecasts based upon the previous year's sales volume, without really factoring in important data such as market trends or technological changes. They've anchored themselves to a number. Professional advisors can be guilty of this when giving you advice. Consider the tale of two financial professionals

— "Advisor A" entered the financial industry in 1985. The first 15 years he was in business, his clients enjoyed a tremendous bull market run. He was employed by one of the large wire-house stock brokerages. "Advisor B" entered the financial industry in 2007. He also worked for a large wire house and received comparable training. However, within the first 12 months of his employment, the clients of Advisor B were rocked by the financial crisis of 2008-2009.

There's a strong likelihood that these two advisors have a different feeling about the stock market, based upon the initial experience they had with it.

Are you guilty of anchoring? Have you ever sold a house? Did how much *you* paid for it enter your mind when you listed the house for sale? The truth of the matter is that what you paid for it years ago had very little to do with what it was worth when you put it up for sale. It's probably safe to say that you have once said "but I paid $____ for it" about something you've sold. Guess what? That's an anchor.

This happens all the time with investments. Investors hold on to investments they shouldn't because they've anchored themselves to a specific price. Let's suppose you bought XYZ stock for $100 per share 10 years ago. It's trading for $50 today. Can you see yourself saying "Let's wait until it gets back to $80 before we sell." You've anchored yourself to the original $100 per share purchase price. The fact of the matter is that if XYZ stock is something you should no longer own, what you paid for it should carry no weight in the decision.

Investing can be very emotional. Let logic and reason overrule emotion when it comes to these kinds of decisions.

Remove the Anchor

Anchoring can happen with any decision you make, and the effects of them have been well documented in thousands of experiments over the years. The important thing is to recognize these anchors and see to it that they don't adversely cloud your judgment and impair your decision-making.

Consider the following techniques when evaluating decisions:

- When working with others, be careful to avoid anchoring yourself by revealing too much information. This is especially true when working with professionals. Let's use real estate agents as an example. If you are trying to sell your house, be careful not to reveal what your asking price is before they share with you what they think your house is worth. If you reveal your price, they may be prone to anchor to it when providing you with their suggested list price.
- Consult with yourself first. Before you allow others to anchor you to their ideas, form your own ideas first. Remain open-minded. Recognize if you've anchored yourself (or been influenced by someone else). Allow yourself to view the problem or decision from different perspectives.

Lastly, and this is especially true in personal finance, reframe the decision by changing the way you ask the question.

For example, financial advisors are often asked questions like:

"I own $10,000 of XYZ stock ... should I sell it?"

As an investor, it's wise to reframe the question ... Ask yourself, "If I had $10,000 sitting in my bank account, would I use that to buy XYZ stock?"

If the answer is "no" to the last question, then the answer to the first question is most likely "yes." There are always tax considerations, but do you see how reframing the question can be helpful? An investor may become anchored to their stock and the original price they paid for it.

Dr. Sigmund Freud's Iceberg Theory

Dr. Sigmund Freud was one of the biggest contributors to the psychology of the mind. In fact, understanding Dr. Freud's iceberg theory could help us make better financial decisions.

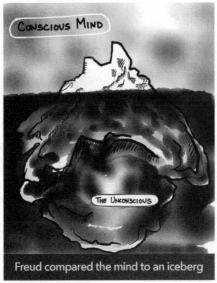

Freud compared the mind to an iceberg

Source: USA Financial

According to Freud, the mind can be broken into three components or levels of awareness.

The first component is the **conscious mind**. This includes everything that we are aware of and can think and talk about rationally. What you are thinking about right now is lodged in the conscious mind.

The second level of awareness is known as the **preconscious mind**. This contains information that is just below the surface of awareness. It is retrieved with relative ease. This level of awareness is usually referred to as our memory.

The third level of awareness is the **unconscious mind**. The unconscious contains thoughts, memories, emotions, and desires that are buried deep inside of us. Many of these thoughts, according to Freud, are unacceptable or unpleasant. They include feelings of pain, anxiety, or conflict.

What does this have to do with making good or bad financial decisions?

Much like an iceberg, we aren't aware of the size and power of what is beneath the surface. The unconscious mind contains significant and sometimes disturbing information that may adversely affect our decision-making. The unconscious harbors memories of events and situations that may have happened to you long ago.

Perhaps as a child, you heard your parents fight about money — this could be buried deep in the unconscious mind. You may have heard your parents or other role models talk positively or negatively about the stock market. Maybe you wanted an expensive toy as a child and were told it was too expensive but without an important discussion occurring about money.

Many people are not certain why they have anxiety about making bigger financial decisions and are surprised to find out that the reason is buried deep in their unconscious mind. This can happen when past experiences make conflicting demands with present desires. It's not uncommon for us to use defense mechanisms to justify these kinds of decisions.

The key to overcoming this is to begin a self-evaluation process to identify the real root of why you feel the way you do about money. Ask yourself if there is more to a financial decision than simply surface-level reasoning. You might be surprised.

It took me a long time to do this soul searching. My parents fought frequently about financial matters — from how to make ends meet to how to invest and spend the extra dollars they had. I believe this childhood experience led me to do what I do today. I've built a business out of helping people accumulate, preserve, and distribute all that they worked so hard to acquire. As I made financial decisions, it was important for me to take into consideration what may be buried deep in my unconscious mind.

One of the issues I personally dealt with was letting go of an issue my parents had with money. They were constantly afraid about not having enough money. As a result of that fear, I think it made them fear the concept of acquiring a lot of wealth. It took a little while for me to realize that my unconscious mind had stored up so many negative conversations between them that I was afraid of being successful. Once I learned how to let the conversations go that I had overheard in my youth, this transformation helped me to make better financial decisions with my conscious mind. This knowledge gave me more confidence to make and keep more wealth.

The $10 Million Question — It's Just Math!

What would you rather have: $1 million handed to you today or a penny today that will double every day for 30 days? If you understand this concept, it will help you understand the compounding effect of money. A penny doubled every day for 30 days is $10,737,418.24.

Albert Einstein once quipped "Compound interest in the eighth wonder of the world. He who understands it, earns it ... he who doesn't ... pays it."

Those who understand this remarkable creative force of compounding interest can create huge financial rewards in your retirement years.

To help you understand this power of compound interest, let me explain it to you in this true story. Mary Jo is a mother of three children and wife to a hard-working husband. Her husband served in World War II and came home with health problems and could never fully resolve them. After 20 years or so working for the Veterans Administration, he ended up getting to know the VA hospital from the customer's point of view.

At age 41, Mary Jo's husband passed away. She continued to work for 35 years as an administrative assistant in a church while raising her family. She cooked, washed clothes, provided for her family and never complained. She never drank and always seemed to have a smile on her face. Her children eventually moved out of the house to start lives of their own. Mary Jo kept the house and got by with the bare necessities. Some years later her children talked with her and expressed concern that she would not have enough money during her retirement years. Mary Jo listened with great love and pride as they spoke.

She told her children not to worry because she had saved a couple million dollars. Her children stared at her in amazement and asked how she could have saved so much. She simply smiled and said she never lived beyond her means and consistently saved and invested the money. It was not something she felt she needed to say or brag about to anyone. All those years working every day, going about her life, taking care of her children, living in that little house, and she had been quietly saving. Consistently and persistently. No one noticed she was a millionaire in the making.

It is too often I see people living beyond their means. People want to have what the neighbor has next door. And to get it, they are willing to overextend themselves and use credit cards while not taking the time to consistently save money. The cost of waiting is a serious discipline that we should all develop more of. A simple daily, weekly, or monthly discipline of saving can help you buy your financial freedom.

This act of discipline seems so simple and easy to do — save a few bucks a day, a few hundred a month, or a few thousand a year. The unfortunate thing is, it is also easy not to do. The mistake of not saving money consistently puts people on a path that will not help them achieve the retirement of their dreams. Successful people make a habit of doing things unsuccessful people won't do.

People Don't Plan to Fail — They Fail to Plan

You skip a day at the gym — no big deal! You eat a high-calorie hamburger. What's the concern? Success and positive results come from making any wise decision, including financial ones. Don't listen to the voice in your head that says, "What I do right now doesn't really matter."

It does matter. It matters every day. Good decision-makers understand that the small choices they make do matter over time. Making smart and wise (albeit small) decisions repeatedly will help create the compounding effect of wealth.

Most people can get caught up with today that they can't see ahead a week or two. Success and wealth are achieved by a willingness to do the things today that may take years to accomplish.

Do you remember the marshmallow test discussed earlier? Those that were able to delay gratification enjoyed more than those that weren't able to demonstrate this ability. If you want to achieve financial success, it's likely that you'll need to delay spending a dollar today in order to enjoy $2 tomorrow.

Also, look to the future and commit long term. Don't make purchases that will make you happy in the short term. Money can control you or you can control money. Take the time to learn from all of your decisions. Commit today by making good financial decisions, however small they may be. They may help you make bigger ones that are more financially rewarding.

As the saying goes, "Rome wasn't built in a day." Your dream retirement (or whatever financial goal you are pursuing) won't be accomplished overnight. One unwise financial decision can affect hundreds of wise ones. You can create powerful results in your financial life by using the tools you hold within you. Take control.

Chapter 3

One Thing Leads to Another —
The Tax Domino Effect

By James Hartwell, CPA, CFP

In this world, nothing can be said to be certain, except death and taxes.
— Benjamin Franklin

Nobody likes to pay taxes. We don't like paying them during our working years, and we dislike paying them when we retire. The difference is the consequence we face in each respective time period. During our working years, we generally pay taxes out of an income stream that is generated from our personal efforts. We work for our money, and out of that money we have to give some of it back to Uncle Sam.

During retirement, a significant portion of our cash flow is generated from our asset base, which may suffer as a result of paying too much in taxes. Tax planning for the retiree is a critical component in the preservation of your hard-earned money — and this planning starts long before your retirement date.

In my experience, the single most important aspect of tax planning for retirees hinges on the management of income. The combined impact of various forms of income, coupled with the lack of meaningful deductions, often result in a higher effective tax rate than what was actually being paid during the working years. Careful planning during your retirement years as to the source of your income can significantly reduce your immediate taxation, preserving more of your wealth for future use.

Stories impact our lives. They impart lessons that, when applicable to your situation, are not quickly forgotten. The stories that are related throughout this chapter are drawn from my experiences as a practicing CPA (Certified Public Accountant) over a period of 30 years. Actual names and circumstances were changed to preserve confidentiality, but the examples are real and happened to real people. The common theme throughout all the stories is the importance of thinking things through, making a plan, and consulting with professionals when appropriate. Your hard-earned wealth is too important to leave to uninformed decision-making.

Meet Andrew

Andrew was a hard-working individual who ran a successful community-based business. This business provided for his family and was eventually sold off so he and his wife could enjoy a well-earned retirement. Andrew minimized the taxes he paid on the sale of his business because he planned ahead and worked with his tax advisor. After the sale, life was good and in many ways much simpler. Andrew went back to planning for and preparing his taxes on his own. One day, after filing his state and federal tax returns, his wife Peggy remarked to him that it certainly felt like they were paying more in taxes than they did during their working years. Through gentle prodding, she convinced him to make an appointment with me at my office.

I met with Andrew and Peggy and reviewed their prior tax returns. As I reviewed, I made sure to ask them about the source of the income and the purpose of each pot of money, or put another way, their underlying assets. I quickly discovered that they were not spending all of the income that was being generated from their assets. In fact, they were adding funds to their savings account every month. We scheduled a follow-up meeting so I could give tax recommendations and look into some planning opportunities using some deferral options available at that time.

Our next meeting proved to be very productive (and profitable) for them. Strategic decisions were made that reduced their federal taxes from $13,000 to $1,200, a savings of $11,800.

Results of tax planning will vary and depends on individual's earnings and specific circumstances.

How This Was Accomplished

We transitioned assets that were providing an income stream that was being taxed as ordinary income tax rates. These assets were transitioned to financial instruments that enjoyed tax-deferred growth. In addition, we sold certain assets that would benefit from the (then) current long-term capital gain tax rate.

Once we identified their annual income needs, Andrew and Peggy lived off of a combination of Social Security and various cash and other short-term assets that were paying very little in earnings (thus, incurring less in taxes). This approach effectively reduced the amount of taxation paid at the ordinary income tax rates and reduced the amount of taxable income generated on their Social Security benefits. We continued this approach over many years.

Lessons to Be Learned

The first lesson is that every asset should have a purpose, and the tax consequence of that asset needs to be clearly understood. Different assets generate different tax consequences. Interest-bearing accounts, such as savings accounts and non-municipal, interest-bearing bonds can generate ordinary interest income. This income is typically taxed at a higher marginal rate than long-term capital gains that may be generated from the sale of a mutual fund, stock, or similar asset.

Many people are surprised to learn that the mutual funds they own may be generating income taxes without them even realizing it. This can be true whether you actually sell the mutual fund or continue to own it. The managers of these funds may be generating capital gains taxes in your account that may adversely impact other aspects of your overall tax and investment plan.

Retirement income is about how much you get to keep — not how much you make.

The second lesson to learn from this story is often overlooked — it has to do with lifestyle. Do you know how much money you need to enjoy the lifestyle you want to enjoy in retirement? Knowing this answer is the first step in retirement income planning. While understanding lifestyle and income needs is important in all stages of our lives, it is especially important when we enter retirement, as it is our asset base that will most likely pay the taxes we incur for the lifestyle we choose.

With the clients of our firm, we use an approximate budget approach with clients facing retirement. This is done for a few reasons. First, we want to determine viability of retirement. We want to answer the question, "Can you do it?" Secondly, we then want to look for the most tax-efficient manner of funding retirement. Finally, we evaluate the lifestyle income need and the taxes likely to be incurred in order to calculate how much in real dollars will have to be withdrawn. This is wise cash flow and tax-bracket management. We do this before any investment recommendations could ever be made.

Let's illustrate this concept with an example of withdrawing money from a completely tax-deferred individual retirement account (IRA). This phraseology indicates that there were no non-deductible contributions made, so any money coming out of the IRA would be considered ordinary income. Suppose you need $20,000 of cash flow from your IRA in order to maintain your lifestyle. Assuming very simple facts and an effective combined tax rate of 20% (federal and state), how much would you actually have to withdraw to receive $20,000 in net proceeds?

Let's do the math.

$20,000 / 80% = $25,000 (total income needed)

Multiply $25,000 by 20% and you have $5,000. So you need $25,000 to enjoy a net income of $20,000. A simple concept, but one that almost every retiree has to discover for themselves at some point.

Another factor that a retiree has to consider is the nature of the income he or she receives. Certain types of income received during retirement can cost you more than other types of income.

During retirement, ordinary taxable income is income that often comes from other sources for the average retiree. Your situation may be different and the following list is not even close to being inclusive but rather it is given as a means of generating thoughtful discussion with your advisors. Forms of income that are considered ordinary income are interest paid on taxable savings, CDs, money market accounts, certain corporate and governmental bonds, non-qualifying dividends received, taxable mutual fund distributions not qualifying for long-term capital gains treatment, taxable distributions from pensions, IRAs and the taxable portion of Social Security.

How much ordinary income you receive can directly drive your tax bracket into or out of a higher tax bracket than the one you are targeting. That is correct, I specifically stated the marginal tax rate you are targeting. I believe all retirees should target the tax bracket they are comfortable living with. While it may be impossible to avoid all taxation, it is far more satisfying to aim for a target that you are comfortable with, knowing that you managed your money in the most efficient manner, so as to pay the government the least amount possible given your specific circumstances. Planning your ordinary income can help you do that.

Another category of income is that of capital gains. For purposes of this chapter, I am only discussing capital gains and not capital losses, as the rules relating to capital losses are beyond the scope of this general discussion. Capital gain is oftentimes defined as income generated from the sale of capital assets. Common and fairly well understood examples would be the sale of stocks, bonds, mutual funds and similar asset types.

There are generally two classifications as to the types of capital gains. They can be either short term or long term. Short term is generally defined as the sale a capital asset held for less than a year. Tax treatment of this type of gain results in it being treated as ordinary income. Long-term capital gain results from the sale of capital assets sold that were held for more than a year. The difference in tax treatment can be significant. There have been times in the history of our tax law when the ordinary marginal tax rate was at 90%. There have been times when in certain circumstances, the tax rate on long-term capital gains has been zero. The difference at any given time can translate into thousands of dollars of tax savings with proper planning. This becomes very significant to a retirees' asset management strategy. Rules are always changing in this area and require careful study and consideration.

Meet Donna

Donna's husband had passed away, and before he died they had purchased together many U.S. savings bonds. She and her husband were somewhat creatures of habit. These bonds were easy to purchase, and they were a "comfortable" investment for them. She and her husband had lived a frugal (and conservative) lifestyle. It was important to Donna to make sure she earned at least something on everything she invested. She only spent money on purchases she absolutely needed. She had a small pension income, IRA distributions and miscellaneous other income, all of which barely made some of her Social Security benefits taxable.

The problem was that she wanted to do something else with the money and was concerned that eventually some of the bonds were going to stop accruing interest. This violated her principle of not earning "something" on everything she owned. Her banker informed her of the earnings on each bond and suggested she see her tax advisor.

We met and discovered that we had to be strategic in cashing in those bonds, as each bond redemption resulted in interest income being recognized, which triggered the recognition of income on her Social

Security benefits. Remember that this type of U.S. savings bond did not pay out the interest, rather just continued to grow in value for up to 30 years but then paid nothing after that. Here was the tax consequence to additional ordinary income flowing to her return: Due to the level of interest income generated from the redemptions, she would have to pick up $850 in taxable Social Security benefits for every $1,000 of income generated from bond redemptions, up to a maximum inclusion of 85% in taxable income.

Let's do the math.

$1,000 of taxable interest income yields $850 of taxable Social Security at an effective federal tax rate of 15%.

That translates into additional taxable income of $1,850 which, when taxed at 15% yields an annual tax of $277.50. Now divide the $277.50 by the original taxable interest income of $1,000, and you have an event that actually doubles the marginal tax rate to 27.75% federal.

The inclusion of taxable Social Security benefits is an often under-considered aspect of retirement planning. Many retirees find that they need to pay in estimates from other sources of funds or cover the taxes through federal withholding on the actual benefits paid out to them. Keep this in mind: When you add additional income to your return, you may possibly trigger tax on your Social Security benefits as well.

Filing to receive your Social Security benefits has both tax and financial planning implications. These tax consequences should be enough of a reason for any individual to carefully consider the many different strategies for electing to claim Social Security benefits. There are penalties in the form of reduced benefits for taking your Social Security early, as well as incentives for extending the date beyond your full retirement age that you claim your benefits.

The decision on when to collect Social Security is one that should be made with many different factors in mind, not just taxes. Many retirees may benefit from managing their cash flow by deferring collection of their Social Security while cashing in more of their IRAs and other taxable sources, so as to minimize the long-term tax consequences to income distribution while claiming benefits. Taxes are only a part of the Social Security decision equation — other parts of that equation include (but aren't limited to) your overall health, family health history and your need for cash flow.

Meet Sarah

One of the key concepts to understand about managing your money during retirement is that moving money can oftentimes create a taxable event. Typically speaking, it's hard to undo a move after the fact.

Sarah was upset with a bank she had dealt with over many years. It had changed ownership several times, and she felt that she was just a number. One day she had had enough. She had a fixed annuity for a number of years that she purchased at the bank. The annuity had grown in value over time as the interest was added to the account on a tax-deferred basis. She had left the annuity alone because she liked the interest rate she had been getting. However, the annuity was past the surrender charge and she was angry at the bank.

Sarah had friends who told her they were treated better at the credit union where they did their banking. Sarah decided to cash out the annuity and deposit the funds into her checking account. Shortly thereafter, she closed the checking account and transferred the funds to the local, friendly credit union. The transfer was completed and she decided she liked the annuity and didn't want to change it. She bought another after-tax annuity offered through the credit union.

Let's review the facts. Sarah was a retired taxpayer filing single status and she was receiving Social Security. Only a small part of her Social Security was subject to taxation. Sarah essentially replaced her old annuity with a new one but cashed out the old annuity in the process.

Here is what happened. I prepared the tax return and called Sarah in to review her tax situation, which was significantly different from prior years. I explained that by cashing out the annuity, she had triggered taxation on all the deferred income that had been sheltered in the annuity. I informed her that she could have done a tax-free exchange of the old annuity to the new annuity and avoided all the taxation once she cashed in the annuity. The tax she had to pay was significant because it triggered recognition of 85% of her Social Security.

What is the lesson from this story? What can we draw from it? Act in haste, repent at leisure, especially when dealing with tax-planning issues.

Meet Dennis and Millie

Tax law is continually changing. What is available one year might be unavailable the next. The key to navigating the treacherous waters of the tax code is regular communication for planning purposes with competent tax and financial planning professionals. Tax preparation is not the same as tax planning. Tax preparation is a matter of recording history, with limited ability to change the overall outcome. Tax planning is looking forward and making informed decisions on actions you can take now to have a more tax favorable future.

Dennis and Millie had always wanted to own a business. They were planners and savers, and after many years they settled on a business venture that intrigued them and for which they felt passionate about. They kept me informed about the progress they were making. One day they called for an appointment with me to discuss their decision. At that meeting, they shared that they decided to open the business and move forward with realizing their dream. I knew they would generate significant ordinary tax losses in the first year, but it could be expected to generate a good profit after two years or three at the most. I suggested that once the business was up and running, they convert all their IRAs to a Roth IRA. We agreed that this was the best course of action.

At the end of the year when the numbers were fairly settled, we converted all of their regular IRA over to the Roth. This amounted to roughly $250,000 in income that was included on their tax return, but which was all covered by the first-year loss on their new business — as was expected and anticipated, because of certain depreciation elections available under the tax code. Converting the regular IRA to a Roth IRA meant that all future earnings and income stream from the Roth IRA could potentially be tax free for as long as the funds lasted.

Your ultimate retirement journey depends upon many factors. Some factors you have control over and some you don't. Tax minimization during the retirement years is one aspect you have some control over. You also have significant control, in most cases, of other types of income you choose to receive. You might also be able to control the nature and timing of the income you receive during retirement. Finally, you have the ability to target your retirement income to the marginal tax bracket that best suits your needs and tax tolerance. You ultimately have a large degree of control over your tax future. That control is made available by careful planning, with objectives in mind, and with the assistance of a professional advisor who understands the tax principles involved in your retirement years.

Chapter 4

More or Less?
I'll Take Less.

By John Cindia, CPA, PFS

Plan First, Invest Second™. If there is one thing you remember as you accumulate and manage wealth, this ought to be it. You will find this to be an important directive to follow if you wish to work toward a successful retirement.

Former American judge Learned Hand once commented:

"Over and over again courts have said that there is nothing sinister in so arranging one's affairs as to keep taxes as low as possible. Everybody does so, rich or poor; and all do right, for nobody owes any public duty to pay more than the law demands: taxes are enforced exactions, not voluntary contributions."

If you read that quote carefully, you'll gather the essence of what smart planning is all about. Smart planning is arranging your affairs in such a way as to keep taxes as low as possible. The question becomes — how do we do this?

A powerful way to convey this important message is to use some real life examples that have come across my desk — both as a CPA and as a retirement planner. It is important to be aware of tax consequences when doing any financial or retirement planning. As you begin to anticipate those consequences, you realize there are many nuances to consider when replacing your paycheck during retirement.

This chapter will highlight areas of concern that could impact taxes and will illustrate the most efficient ways to avoid common mistakes. When designing a portfolio, strategy and structure matter. Deciding on what types of investments should be held in certain accounts can be crucial when considering tax impact. Finally, I will alert you to some very basic principles that are routinely overlooked by many investors.

The financial world is full of jargon. Many professionals use their own jargon and simply assume that you know what it means. Before getting too far into it, it might be helpful to provide some definitions of what we will discuss.

1) **"Buckets"** — I have always enjoyed this term for describing a source of funds to be used for various purposes. A bucket is simply a generic reference for an account (or multiple accounts) that should be mentally separated from other accounts.

2) **Qualified and Non-qualified assets** —
   a. **Qualified** — Any asset that is in a pension plan, 401(k), 403(b), IRA, Roth or various other types of savings plans. These may be deductible but defer taxes to a later date or eliminate taxes altogether, if structured properly. The reason the term "qualified" is used is because these accounts "qualify" for special tax-deferral benefits with the IRS.
   b. **Non-qualified** — Accounts that are not tax deferred/tax qualified. Examples include savings accounts, checking accounts or normal brokerage accounts that hold investments. You will receive a 1099 from these accounts at the end of the year to report any taxable transactions from interest, dividends or capital gains.

3) **Wasting asset** — A strategy of using or spending some savings or investments while other assets are allowed to grow. We use time as a strategy to build guarantees for particular types of investments.

4) **Three-legged stool of income** — A concept that likens the basic types of income to a three-legged stool. If any leg of the stool is weak or missing, the stool will collapse. These legs represent the following:
   a. Pension or 401(k) assets
   b. Social Security
   c. Personal savings and investments

5) **Bracket creep** — When you move between tax brackets and see a distinct and sometimes significant increase in taxes. An example would be moving from the 15% to 25% tax bracket resulting in an increase of 66% more tax for every dollar in that new tax bracket.

6) **Social Security FRA** — FRA stands for "full retirement age." When you'll receive 100% of your benefit at a certain age, based on your year of birth. If you claim prior to that age, you receive less; if you claim beyond that age, you could receive more benefits.

7) **Risk tolerance** — How much money can you stand to lose or put at risk without having a devastating effect on your savings budget or retirement plan. If you cannot stand to lose much, then you have a low tolerance for risk and should stay in guaranteed or safe investments. If you're in the stock market, then you have a higher risk tolerance and can normally withstand the ups and downs of the market better than a lower risk individual.

What Were They Thinking?

Many people make inaccurate assumptions about their ability to retire and waste precious time and negatively impact their quality of life. This can be avoided by meeting with an experienced financial advisor.

Meet Bill and Susan

Let's start with a couple I began working with a few years back, Bill and Susan. They needed to keep working because they didn't have enough money to retire.

The obvious follow-up question was, "How much do you have and how much have you calculated that you will need?" They sheepishly handed me their statements and said, "We aren't really sure what we have, but we just know it isn't enough to retire on."

I combed through the statements and discovered that Bill and Susan had amassed a little over $1,000,000 (all but $20,000 was in qualified accounts).

As the conversation continued, I pointed out a few concerns and opportunities. Having too much money in one type of tax bucket is a concern. Every dollar that is ever pulled from these accounts will be taxed at some point. This is where some non-qualified dollars could be beneficial for living expenses and emergencies while striving to keep taxes lower and avoid the potential for bracket creep.

Dividends

This may be a good time to explain a couple more terms: Qualified versus non-qualified dividends. Qualified dividends can have a significant impact on taxes. When an individual is in the 10%–15% tax bracket and has actual qualified dividends (meets the holding period and is, for the most part, a domestic U.S. corporation) then the rate on those dividends is zero, nada, zilch, nothing. But, if the dividends are considered non-qualified dividends and are paid from real estate trusts, master limited partnerships, bond mutual funds and some dividends within equity mutual funds, they will be taxed at normal rates of 10%–39.6%.

Having a balance of savings between qualified and non-qualified buckets allows for some additional planning that may potentially result in lower taxes when taking income during retirement. A suggestion to this couple was to defer their 401(k) savings only up to the match of the employer. Since they had little money in an emergency fund (most of the $20,000 was earmarked for a child's wedding and school tuition), I suggested any funds over the deferred match of the employer go toward an emergency fund. They also were under the earnings maximum to set up Roth IRAs. As a result, we started to fund two Roth IRAs. The Roth IRAs gave them additional choices or buckets of money to draw from in retirement.

This strategy gives Bill and Susan more flexibility each year in retirement, which may be beneficial if/when tax laws change.

The lesson that we shared with Bill and Susan was an important one in diversification. Many investors think that diversification only refers to asset classes. Diversification from a tax perspective is equally as important. Having too much money in one type of taxable account, as in Bill and Susan's previous example, may restrict planning opportunities. It can negatively impact your retirement income strategy.

Speaking of income — what happens when you generate substantial dividends and/or interest income from accounts and don't need the income? This can result in paying more in taxes, and many people could benefit from a little planning to shift those assets into tax-deferred or tax-free vehicles. The following is an example.

Meet Jeff and Julia

When I first met Jeff and Julia, they had been retired for several years from the teaching profession. They were both fortunate enough to receive nice pensions from their former employers. They had saved substantial assets that were generating investment returns resulting in interest and dividends.

Jeff and Julia enjoyed a modest lifestyle and lived well within their means. In fact, their monthly expenses were well below their monthly pension income. Their investments were all non-qualified, just the opposite of the previous example we discussed. Their interest and dividends totaled over $30,000 a year. These dividends, not being qualified for favorable tax rates, resulted in normal tax rates due to bracket creep, all of which were pushed to the higher 25% bracket.

As a result, Jeff and Julia were getting hit with a tax bill each and every year on income they weren't even using. The strategy we explored for them was to find vehicles that could reduce or eliminate the taxes they were paying on these accounts. Another important discussion to have was whether this money was considered "live on" money or "leave on" money. In order to find the right option for them, they had to answer this question and determine the true purpose for the money.

These first two examples described are not unusual. In fact, they tend to be the status quo for investors and retirees who haven't drafted a proper plan. All too often I will find clients with several brokerage accounts, different brokers and pension accounts left with old employers. By not coordinating these accounts, tax deferral or tax reduction opportunities may be missed, and investors may pay higher than necessary fees as a result of higher custodial charges on smaller accounts. This failure to coordinate, from a tax perspective, can lead to inefficient portfolios.

A basic tenet of a proper plan is to hold your assets in different buckets. Assets that generate interest or dividend income might be worth owning in qualified accounts like IRAs or 401(k)s to maximize tax efficiency. Compound interest and growth is a powerful concept, and taxes negatively impact that power. If you know that the asset won't be touched for a very long time, consider tax-deferred vehicles. Assets that may benefit from more favorable long-term capital gains tax rates might be more logical for you to own in non-qualified accounts. So right now we have started with two buckets of money, a qualified bucket and a non-qualified bucket. Each has investments we will draw from during retirement to help keep taxes as low as possible.

In this chapter, I want to keep our concentration on the tax consequences and how you may control them better, not on which investment may be best for you. I will, however, suggest types of investments that may work in a certain scenario. Risk tolerance can come into play here as your comfort level with risk will undoubtedly influence the type of investments that make the most sense for you.

How many different buckets should you have? That depends. It is not unusual to have anywhere from four to seven (or more) different types of buckets to pull from. If you have less money to invest, you'll have fewer buckets; if you have more money, you'll have more buckets to diversify for different planning objectives.

We've found that it is helpful for our clients to think in terms of buckets. This concept simplifies their approach to money. Each bucket has a definitive purpose. The type of asset(s) and the tax classification may vary by bucket. In fact, one bucket could include a few different types of investments — from municipal bonds providing tax-free income to a tax-deferred annuity. It's important that the assets are working toward the pre-defined goal of the bucket.

Let's look at a very basic approach to this concept. Each bucket gets assigned a "duty," if you will. Some are for income, some are for growth, and some are for living expenses possibly using wasting assets. (I previously referred to wasting assets, which would allow for investment growth or guarantees to build in other buckets.)

Your buckets could look like this:

Money needed for use in a few days to a year or two:
- Cash
- CDs
- Short-term bonds, normally less than a two-year maturity

This can normally be between three years to seven years:
- Bonds with maturities less than seven years
- Dividend-paying stocks for those who can handle some market fluctuation or volatility
- Longer term CDs
- Fixed annuities can range from two to seven years
- Possibly some indexed annuities used for guaranteed income

To be held for longer than seven years:
- Stocks
- REITS
- Variable annuities
- Indexed annuities
- Bonds
- CDs
- Exchange-traded funds (ETFs)
- Municipal bonds

Here's an example of a typical client we work with.

Meet John and Mary

John and Mary are both 60 years old and aiming to retire at age 65. They each earn approximately $60,000 a year. John has a 401(k) with $500,000 and a Roth IRA with $125,000. Mary has a 403(b) account with her hospital employer that is worth about $250,000. She also owns a Roth IRA valued at $60,000. John has a discount brokerage account with $20,000. Like many clients, John enjoys trading stocks and uses this as his personal "play account." There is also a joint brokerage account, started years ago, with $45,000 of various dividend-paying stocks inherited from Mary's parents. An additional joint savings account exists that acts as an emergency fund worth $25,000.

In this example, we have at least seven buckets of money — two pension plans, two Roth IRAs, one individual brokerage account, one joint brokerage account and one joint savings account. The key to proper planning is to help define the purpose of each one of these buckets. Like a previous example, these clients' assets are heavily skewed toward qualified retirement savings vehicles. This isn't necessarily a bad thing, but it presents specific planning challenges and opportunities. The nice thing is, we have time to plan and they have plenty of planning options.

Upon reviewing their investment statements, I found that most of the accounts had been invested in mutual funds with at least a 75% overlap in similar funds (in some cases there were exact duplicate ownership of funds). There was little diversification amongst asset classes. The question is, "Is that a bad thing?" Maybe, maybe not. There is an underlying element here that has yet to be addressed. RISK!!! What type of risk have they subjected themselves to and are they aware of that risk so close to retirement?

Comprehensive advisors will use sophisticated risk profiles to help truly measure an individual's actual risk tolerance and how it compares with their existing portfolio. This is a starting point for us to determine the types, placement and timing of investments that will get them to their desired retirement goals. The risk model we use employs a scoring range from 1 to 99. The 1 is the safest investment or a guaranteed cash equivalent and 99 is a risky investment, like a volatile individual stock. When we ran this analysis on John and Mary, their respective portfolios came out to a 75 for John and an 83 for Mary, both very aggressive.

Then each took a test showing their personal risk scores. John was a 39 and Mary was a 25. This is a very different scenario from what their portfolios suggested. Can you see a possible disconnect here? John and Mary have a conservative mindset with an aggressive portfolio. This is not an ideal scenario for them. It suggests that they are invested much more aggressively than they have the stomach for. In other words — a significant downturn in the stock market may cause them to react in a way that may not be beneficial to their portfolio.

Let's get back to the tax aspects of John and Mary's portfolio. Upon review and discussion, the plan we moved forward with was to continue to hold the dividend paying stocks, as they were able to benefit from the lowest possible tax brackets in light of their qualified dividend status. John's "play" money was consolidated with the joint account to purchase some additional dividend-paying stocks. We also used a provision within John's 401(k) (known as an in-service distribution) in order to create two different IRA accounts. In light of their more conservative nature, John wanted some more predictability in his portfolio, so he elected to place one of the IRA accounts into a fixed-indexed annuity to allow for stable growth and future income guarantees. The other IRA was placed in a conservative blend of balanced investments. This was done to bring their investments more in line with their risk tolerance.

The planning was not finished yet. In fact, before we could even make any of those investments, we had an important consideration to factor in to the equation for John and Mary — Social Security. This is the first step to retirement income planning.

The Social Security piece of retirement planning is very important from a couple of viewpoints. First, when you make an election prior to your full retirement age (FRA), you are subject to certain earnings limitations. Secondly, you are making a choice that could possibly negatively impact your tax situation if not properly planned for.

Since we knew they both planned to work until age 65, this presented the question of when they should take Social Security. Their FRA is 66, so if they decided to take their benefits at retirement (age 65), they would be accepting a small but permanent reduction. In addition, they would be forfeiting the opportunity to take advantage of some of the strategic claiming strategies available to married couples.

At the time we created the plan (their age 60), it was decided that we would wait until they reached FRA to begin claiming Social Security benefits. This meant that we would take more from personal savings in that first year of retirement. The plan we laid out was to take a strategic (but not yet determined) amount from tax-deferred retirement accounts in order to avoid launching them into the next tax bracket. We've also left the option open to consider waiting to take Mary's Social Security until she turns 70. This might require a slightly higher withdrawal amount from their traditional IRAs, but this planning tactic affords us two potential benefits:

1. Higher lifetime Social Security benefits and income
2. A strategic spending down of traditional IRA money to avoid higher required minimum withdrawals at age 70½

The most important items we stress with our financial plans are flexibility and logic. We strive to ensure our clients have some flexibility within their plans, because it is very rare for one's financial life to go 100% according to plan. Proper planning addresses the "what-ifs" that we may encounter in life. We also want to infuse as much logic into the plan as well. When you understand your plan, you're much more likely to stick with it. John and Mary were blessed. They had ample assets to help them meet their financial goals. As a result, they found they could invest more conservatively (and in accordance with their risk profile). In other words, they found they didn't need to achieve big returns (thus taking on bigger risks) in order to accomplish their retirement goals.

Plan First, Invest Second. Do you recall those words at the beginning of this chapter? It is the basis of each plan created. If you use that premise throughout your planning, you will be on the path toward a more successful transition to retirement. If you don't understand how an investment fits into the bigger picture — don't invest in it. Knowledge is power!

Chapter 5

IRA Tax Traps to Avoid

By Earl Schultz, ChFC, CLU

Note: The examples used in this chapter are based upon IRS rules, regulations, and tax rates at the time of publishing.

The topic of individual retirement accounts (IRAs), their associated taxes, and potential penalties may be as vast as the oceans around the world and as difficult as navigating an unfamiliar and dark jungle on a solo excursion. Suppose you were to embark on this type of excursion. Let's assume you had four choices to help you through the jungle. You could:

A. Download an app onto your smartphone to help navigate.
B. Print a hard copy of a jungle map.
C. Enlist the services of a knowledgeable guide.
D. Buy an encyclopedia of jungle animals and plants and their respective dangers.

Given these four choices, what feels most comfortable? I would guess that most people feel confident having a knowledgeable guide by their side, someone who has helped others navigate that same jungle.

This same example can be applied to your navigation of the world of IRAs. There are many dangers and tax traps to avoid. You can read books like this one, conduct internet searches on the topic, browse through numerous publications, and even attend several educational seminars. Each of these options can help, and acquiring knowledge is never wasted. However, I believe your best option is to seek the wisdom and guidance of an experienced professional who recognizes the importance of handling IRA transactions with care.

To comprehensively cover the topic of IRAs, it would indeed require volumes, not just a book chapter. As a result, our focus is to explore some of the most common tax traps that routinely catch investors by surprise. Remember, these discussions will be far from all-inclusive. Before making any moves with your IRAs, I encourage you to meet with a professional who is knowledgeable on the subject.

There are several types of IRAs that can be established by an investor: traditional, Roth, the simplified employee pension (SEP) plan, and the savings investment match plan for employees (SIMPLE). The traditional and Roth IRA are by far the most common. The SEP and the SIMPLE are retirement accounts linked to your employment. We will not cover the rules regarding how much money can be contributed to SEP or SIMPLE IRAs. The money invested into your SEP is actually contributed by the employer. With a SIMPLE IRA, contributions can be made by the employee or employer or a combination of both. For the most part, taxes on both of these IRAs are the same as for the traditional IRA. There is an additional trap in the form of a substantial penalty, however, if money is moved out of a SIMPLE IRA within a specified period of time, but we will leave that topic for another time.

Traditional vs. Roth

To start off, let's examine the major differences between a traditional and Roth IRA. With a traditional IRA, any money invested within a given tax year provides you a tax deduction for that amount on your tax return. In other words, you will not pay tax on the amount invested that year, and you will not have to pay tax each year on the gains within that IRA as it grows. This does not mean that the IRA is tax-free, however, it means that the taxes are only deferred while the money remains within the traditional IRA. When you reach your retirement years and begin withdrawing money from that IRA, all of it will be considered taxable income. This brings us to one potential trap already. That is, we don't know at what rate that money will be taxed when it is withdrawn years later. Most people believe that tax rates will be higher in the future, and if that is so, deferring taxes at a rather low rate may result in paying taxes at a much higher rate in the future.

Money invested in a given tax year into a Roth IRA does not receive any immediate tax favoritism. It's money invested on an after-tax basis. One advantage to this is that you pay tax before you invest it, and it won't be taxed when you withdraw it later. What happens to the growth of that money in future years, you may be wondering. Therein lies the real beauty of the Roth IRA. All future gains can be withdrawn in retirement completely tax-free. Let me say that in a different way. The taxes on this IRA are not deferred, and you will not pay them later. Rather, there will not be any tax on qualified distributions in the future.

Let's look at a simple example that may clarify this tax difference. Consider the case of a farmer who wants to buy seed to plant hundreds of acres of crop for harvesting later, but the cost of the seed is $10,000 for the entire crop. After the crop matures and is harvested, the sale of that produce will return $200,000. What if the IRS comes knocking at the door and offers him two options on how to pay the tax due? The first option is to take a $10,000 tax deduction that year for the cost of the seed, but in return he must pay tax on the entire $200,000. The second option will provide him no tax benefit whatsoever on the $10,000 he paid (he will have to pay tax), but there is no tax due on the $200,000.

In option one, the farmer pays no tax on the seed but is fully taxed on the harvest. In option two, he is taxed on the seed but receives the proceeds from the harvest tax-free. Put yourself in the shoes of the farmer. Would you rather pay tax on the seed or the harvest?

With the traditional IRA you are being taxed on the harvest. With a Roth IRA you are being taxed on the seed only.

This story illustrates the tremendous potential tax difference between the traditional and the Roth IRA. The SEP and SIMPLE IRAs would also be taxed in the same manner as the traditional IRA.

Capital Gains

Different kinds of income can be taxed at different rates. Traditional IRAs are often invested in stocks or mutual funds. These types of investments generate capital gains income; individual stocks, when they are sold; and mutual funds when stocks within the funds are sold by the fund company. If the sales of stock occur after the stocks were held for more than one year, the capital gains are considered "long-term gains." If stocks are sold prior to one year after purchase, the capital gains are labeled "short-term gains."

Long-term gains receive favorable tax treatment, but only if the stocks being sold are outside of an IRA. If the investments are within the IRA, this reduced tax rate on long-term gains is forfeited. Short-term gains are taxed at the same rate as ordinary income and, therefore, don't receive any special tax-rate benefit. To find out what the current tax rates are, check the IRS website. The TurboTax and Motley Fool websites also do a nice job of explaining short- and long-term capital gains.[1]

Limitations on Contributions

It is important to note that there are limitations on how much money you can contribute each year. For 2017, if you are under the age of 50 you are limited to a total investment of $5,500 per person in either the traditional IRA, the Roth IRA, or any combination of the two. If, on the other hand, you are greater than 50 years of age, or are turning age 50 in the current tax year, there is an additional $1,000 catch-up provision allowed by the IRS meaning that you can contribute up to $6,500 per year into either or a combination of both. These amounts are updated periodically by the IRS, so visit its website for updated information.[2]

If you intentionally or inadvertently contribute more than the allowed amount during a year, the additional amount will incur a penalty equal to 6% of that excess contribution each year that it remains in the account. Correcting an excess contribution must be done in a timely manner to avoid the penalty. The amount in excess must be removed from the IRA along with any earnings realized. The IRA custodian must be informed that this distribution is a return of an excess contribution. Individuals would have until October 15 of the following year to correct it. Any gain distributed with the excess contribution will be taxable and will also be subject to the 10% early distribution penalty if under age 59½.[3]

Not understanding these tax differences can trap you into paying more in taxes than necessary. This tax trap is far more reaching than what one would assume from just reading the above. Indeed, when having to pay tax on IRA withdrawals during retirement, the tax can be like a creeping vine that works its way into other areas of your retirement planning. For example, the degree to which your Social Security benefits will be taxed during retirement is dependent upon your other sources of income at that time. This is important to understand because it means that if you are taking withdrawals from a traditional IRA in retirement, it can cause up to 85% of your Social Security to be considered taxable income. Taking distributions from a Roth IRA, on the other hand, will not cause your Social Security to be taxed.[4] This insidious creeping vine has now worked its way not only through your traditional IRA but also to your Social Security benefits.

Required Minimum Distributions — Age Matters

Any money invested into a traditional IRA on a pre-tax basis (when you receive a tax deduction on that amount) is essentially locked up until age 59½. If you withdraw that money prior to 59½, you will not only be taxed on it as an addition to your other taxable income for the year but will also incur a 10% IRS penalty.[5] Yes, there are some exceptions to that rule such as a withdrawal used for a first-time home purchase. But be aware that for most withdrawals prior to that age, the IRS will come after you for that tax and penalty.

The second age of great significance with the traditional IRA is 70½. The year in which you turn 70½, you are required to begin taking required minimum distributions (RMD) from your traditional IRA (the rules for the SEP and SIMPLE IRAs are the same). Each year the IRS will use the balance of each account on December 31 of the prior year and divide that balance by a number from an IRS table that determines how much money you must withdraw from the IRA in this new year. The percentage that must be withdrawn increases each year.[6]

While this may not sound so bad initially, it can be a huge tax trap in the future. Many retirees find that the amount of income they must claim as taxable each year far exceeds the amount of income they need for living expenses. This means that they may be thrown into a higher tax bracket because of having to withdraw all this extra taxable income, and as mentioned earlier, it almost certainly means their Social Security will have to be taxed at the maximum amount. This is one of the reasons why proper planning before retirement is absolutely essential. You need to have a plan that will assign a job description to each of your investments so that you know how and when they will be used and in conjunction with what other sources of income. Surely we all have as our goal to be financially prepared for retirement. It's been said, however, that a goal without a plan is merely a wish.

What is the consequence of forgetting to take your RMD? Many people wait until late in the year because it's not necessary that it be taken until the end of the year. What's the problem? Well, I've seen it happen all too often. Thanksgiving comes along, Christmas preparations have begun, and we forget to take the RMD from our IRA. This is where the IRS will really hammer you. The penalty for not taking the RMD in any given year is 50% of that amount, and you still also need to pay the tax.[7] Check the IRS website for more information.

The Roth IRA is a bit different as it's not subject to RMDs. You will never need to take an RMD from your Roth IRA at any age. It only applies while the owner is alive.[8] But what happens if you pass away and your spouse takes over that IRA in his or her name, commonly known as a spousal rollover? Must your spouse ever take an RMD from that IRA during his or her lifetime? The answer is no. The rules for your spouse would be exactly the same as the rules for you when you owned the Roth.

Now let's take it one step further. What happens when your spouse passes away, assuming that your children were named as beneficiaries and they decide to roll that account into a properly titled inherited Roth IRA for their benefit(s)? Must your children ever take RMDs on this inherited Roth IRA? To the surprise of many people, the answer is yes. "But wait just a moment," you may be thinking. "I thought Roth IRAs were always exempt from this." In actuality, the IRS says that Roth IRAs are exempt from RMDs for both the owner and a spousal beneficiary. Non-spousal beneficiaries must take an RMD each year beginning the year after death of the previous owner. The good news is that because it's a Roth IRA, the distributions are still tax-free. But here's another tax trap. If your children inherit a Roth IRA and failed to realize that they must begin taking RMDs each year, it's possible that they won't do so. For each year's RMD that they miss, there is a 50% penalty on the amount they failed to take.[9]

Rollovers and Transfers

We are living in an age where most people have an employer-sponsored retirement plan. Most of these plans are what we referred to as defined contribution plans, the most common of which are a 401(k) and 403(b). These workplace plans are most typically rolled over into one or more traditional IRAs at retirement, if not earlier as part of an "in-service distribution" rollover. In addition, many people own IRA accounts that may also be moved to a different IRA. Not knowing how to properly move the money in either situation, you'll find yourself in another tax trap.

The first, and generally the simplest approach, to moving money from a workplace retirement plan into an IRA is a direct rollover from the plan to the IRA. The plan custodian makes a check payable to the new custodian and only the new custodian can endorse and cash that check. This absolves the owner from being unexpectedly taxed or penalized.

The second is known as a 60-day rollover or non-direct rollover. The custodian of the workplace retirement plan sends the owner a check made payable in the owner's name. The owner can cash the check and within 60 days avoid being fully taxed by depositing the proceeds to the new IRA.

Transfers are similar to rollovers in that a direct transfer is also the simplest approach and accomplished by having the custodian of the existing IRA make a check payable directly to the custodian of the new IRA. An example of how to make payable is: "Trust Company of America FBO Jane Smith." Having the check made payable in this manner prevents all unexpected taxes and penalties that could otherwise be levied upon the account owner. In other words, it completely takes away the risk.

The second is a 60-day transfer, sometimes still referred to as a 60-day rollover. The current IRA custodian makes the check payable directly to you. When you receive the check, deposit it and write a new check from your checking account payable to the new custodian. You must get this check to the new custodian within 60 days from the time you received the initial check. Failing to do so will render the full value of that IRA taxable in that tax year. If this happens, you are not only losing the amount of tax you have to pay but also the future growth that may have occurred on that money had it not been paid out to taxes.

A couple of potential tax traps can happen though with a rollover. First, in non-directly rolling over the money, because the plan custodian is making the check payable to the owner, he is required to withhold 20% of the total value of the plan for federal tax in case the entire 100% is not rolled over. The owner will receive a check from his plan for only 80% of the plan value. When the owner cashes that check and deposits it into the new IRA, he will only be effectively rolling over 80% of the initial account value. The 20% is withheld, cannot be rolled over and will be fully taxable that year. To avoid the tax on that 20%, the owner must come up with the amount of money equal to the 20% withheld from another source of funds. What if you don't have that 20% available to invest from other funds? Well, then you're out of luck and that 20% that was never reinvested in the new plan is now taxable income, and subject to any penalties.[10]

The second tax trap you could incur by non-directly rolling this money over would be in not getting the money into the IRA within 60 days. If you were to have a significant event occur in your life that took your attention away from investing this check, or if you forgot about it and the 60 days passed, the entire amount would be added to all other sources of taxable income for that tax year, and you must include the amount as income on your tax return.[11] The best advice here is to have a knowledgeable, licensed IRA professional help guide you through these transactions.

The Once-Per-Year Rollover Rule

Up until a new tax court ruling in 2014, it was possible to take money out of one IRA, then within 60 days put it back in by withdrawing money out of a second IRA, and within another 60 days, pay that money back to the second IRA by withdrawing money out of a third IRA. There was no limit to how many times this could be done or over what period, effectively allowing a tax- and penalty-free withdrawal over an indefinite period. The tax court ruled that the IRS' interpretation of the once-per-year rollover rules were incorrect and replaced those with the new stricter interpretation. Beginning in 2015, the new rule states that IRA owners can only do one 60-day IRA-to-IRA rollover within a 12-month period. An IRA owner can only make one tax-free, 60-day rollover from one IRA to another IRA (or the same) in any one-year period, regardless of the number of IRAs owned. The one-year clock begins ticking on the day the IRA distribution is received. Visit the IRS website to read more about this rule.[12]

Example: Marty owns a traditional IRA with ABC mutual fund company. He withdraws money on April 1, 2015, and deposits it into a new IRA with XYZ bank on May 30, 2015, which is within the 60-day allowable time frame. After this transaction, Marty cannot roll over an amount from any of his IRAs into another until after April 1, 2016, one year from April 1, 2015.

Note: For purposes of this rule, an owner's traditional and Roth IRAs, as well as SIMPLE and SEP IRAs, are all combined and treated as one. The fact that Roth IRAs are treated differently for tax purposes makes no difference. In other words, Roth IRAs are combined with all of someone's non-Roth IRAs. It's important to understand the vast tax implications of violating this new rule.[13] Again, visit the IRS website to read more.

And, if that's not bad enough, the fact that your IRA becomes immediately taxable can cause you to lose the personal exemptions you normally get on your tax return depending on the amount of your taxable income for the year. You can see how one tax trap can snowball into another, and the amount of tax owed can multiply.

Direct transfers of IRA money are not limited, and the one-rollover-per-year rule applies only to 60-day rollovers.[14]

Estate Considerations

What happens to your IRA during the distribution years and at the time of an inheritance may be one of the largest tax traps you could encounter.

Let's assume that John Tyler owns a traditional IRA with a substantial balance when he passes. Hopefully, John has been rightfully advised to ensure he has primary beneficiaries listed and also, generally, contingent beneficiaries. If he has not listed any, the tax trap is enormous because the IRA will go into probate and become taxable and subject to probate costs, in addition to the tax. Depending on the size of the estate, the IRA could also be hit with substantial estate tax. Total taxes and probate fees on a large estate could mean that more than 75% of the IRA could be lost. The simple lesson here is that properly naming primary and contingent beneficiaries is of extreme importance in preserving your IRAs for the next generation.[15]

Now let's assume that John has properly named his two children, Mike and Emily, as his primary beneficiaries and to share equally. This is great, but it doesn't mean that the IRA is clear of all tax traps. Depending on the actions of Mike and/or Emily, much of this IRA can still be lost. They both have choices to make in how to receive their shares, and one is calling the custodian of the account and asking that their shares be liquidated and sent to them. This could mean at tax time, they may be finding they owe tens, hundreds or thousands of dollars in taxes for that year. A call would no doubt go out to the accountant asking, "How can we avoid having to pay all this tax?" The answer is that they can't. They made a huge mistake and must now pay for it.

On the other hand, Mike and Emily may be aware that they can keep this money in an IRA and continue to defer the taxes, but they are unsure of how to do this. Mike decides that he will take the money out of the account and roll it into a new IRA in his name within 60 days because he heard there might be tax benefits. Unfortunately, what Mike didn't understand is that to continue to defer the tax, the money must be transferred into a properly titled inherited IRA. Proper titling for an inherited IRA would be as follows: "John Tyler (deceased mm/dd/20xx) Inherited IRA FBO Michael Tyler." This new IRA actually remains in the name of the deceased owner for the benefit of the beneficiary. Failing to transfer this money into an inherited IRA will result in full taxation of the IRA value in the year of liquidation. Furthermore, if any or all of that money is invested in an IRA in only Mike's name, the IRS will consider it as an excess contribution, which will incur a 6% penalty for each year the money remains in that account going forward.[16]

The bottom line is that the beneficiary(ies) should always be informed that when the account owner dies, they should touch absolutely nothing until they have consulted a qualified IRA professional to learn about all their options and the tax consequences of each.

It has been my experience in working with individuals and families that most of them focus their attention on growing their IRAs until they feel comfortable they'll have enough money to retire. Others don't look far enough ahead. People are generally in one of three situations.

1. There won't be enough money in either the IRAs or non-qualified accounts to sustain them through their life expectancy. Not a good place to be, for sure.
2. There may be enough money but with little or nothing left over after death.
3. Individuals and families who have been successful in growing a substantial nest egg have enough to last through retirement, and there's enough left over for the next generation.

As was mentioned earlier, one of the major tax problems with IRAs is that while we know how much we're saving in taxes in the year we take a tax deduction, assuming a traditional IRA investment, we have no idea at what rate our distributions will be taxed in the future. Let's explore another example to make this clear.

Suppose you need a mortgage for a new home purchase. You visit the local bank and the banker tells you the monthly amount you'll be required to pay back, but the interest rate on the mortgage is open ended. The banker says the bank has the right to change the interest rate on the amortization schedule at any time. What may be a 4% interest rate today could end up being a 10% interest rate before the mortgage is paid off. With this fluctuation and potential increase, would you accept it? The answer is of course no! We should not consider a mortgage without clear terms.

But now think about this for a moment. Isn't that exactly what we're doing with traditional, SIMPLE, and SEP IRAs? Since we have no idea what the tax rate will be on distributions from these accounts in the future, it's really no different than having an open-ended interest rate on a mortgage. What if you deferred taxes on your IRA contributions today saving you 15%, for example, and are then taxed later on a much larger amount at a rate of possibly 30%? To take it a step further, what if you're taxed on that entire IRA at 40%? With our outstanding of federal debt and the more than $70 trillion in unfunded liabilities this country carries, none of us knows what the tax rates will be 10, 20, or 30 years from now.

It could be very costly in your later retirement years, but the ones who suffer the most may be your children. Most people say that they don't want the government to get any more money from their wealth than is absolutely necessary, yet those same people have generally failed to take any action to protect that wealth.

The good news is there are many strategies available that will allow you to provide a degree of protection for your wealth. Some of those strategies involve various types of trusts, however, many other strategies do not. Strategies may involve partial conversions to Roth IRAs, life insurance, or a combination of both.

Here's another example. You have an IRA worth $500,000 and plan to withdraw a certain percentage of the account value each year. Depending on what that percentage is, your IRA may gradually decrease in value through the years. When you pass away, your spouse or children withdraw the money but will continue to owe tax every year at an unknown tax rate for as long as the money lasts, or it will incur a substantial tax bite on the lump sum taken. What you weren't told when you were advised to fund the IRAs for your retirement is that a $500,000 IRA may really only be worth $350,000, because the remainder is a tax trap that will go to funding the government. Indeed, your portion could be even smaller.

With proper strategy planning, it may be possible for you to withdraw a substantial percentage from your account every year throughout your retirement and for as long as you live, yet still leave the full $500,000 initial balance to your beneficiary(ies) completely tax-free. Think about that for a moment. You are living off a substantial amount of the IRA and paying tax on only your withdrawals but still leaving the initial full balance of it to your heirs 100% tax-free. Even if you weren't loved during life, you certainly will be during death. This strategy has been referred to as an "IRA rescue" technique.

Have you ever wondered how the wealthiest people in the United States protect their wealth from an unnecessary amount of government interference? They use a number of different wealth-protecting strategies. Life insurance is one of the most common strategies but not the only one. Many wealthy people purchase life insurance at pennies on the dollar, effectively leveraging their investment to provide a much larger tax-free benefit to their heirs to pay off income taxes, probate, and even estate taxes so that the value of their estate can go to their heirs without burden.

The number of wealth-protecting strategies available is quite large. The purpose of this chapter is not to provide a comprehensive knowledge of all possible strategies, but rather to make you aware that by working with a knowledgeable professional it may be possible to save large amounts for your heirs as opposed to saving it for the government.

Chapter 6

The Roth IRA — To Convert or Not Convert?

By William J. LaCasse, ChFC, RFC

Note: The examples used in this chapter are based upon IRS rules, regulations, and tax rates at the time of publishing.

Most every financial professional has an opinion on the conversion from a traditional IRA to a Roth IRA. As with most opinions, they vary from the extreme of "No, never convert" to "Yes, always convert" and all options in between.

You have probably noticed a theme in this book — *plan first and invest second*. When it comes to the Roth IRA conversion, you should always plan first, and convert second. As with all other investment decisions, there is no one-size-fits-all answer. It is imperative that you understand the underlying issues and options and how they may affect your own needs and desires. Putting these pieces of the puzzle together will help you as you assess the Roth IRA conversion decision, especially as it relates to the short-term versus long-term tax ramifications.

Before we get into the why or why not of converting, it will help to have a better understanding of the rules, especially those relating to tax laws. Contributing to a Roth IRA is different than converting a traditional IRA to a Roth IRA. There are maximum limits on how much you can contribute to a Roth IRA for the first time. However, there aren't limits on how much you can convert from a traditional IRA to a Roth IRA. This is a key point, as it provides you with greater flexibility in planning.

There are three basic ways to convert to a Roth IRA:

1. *Same Trustee Transfer.* This is where the money stays at the same financial institution. You would simply establish a Roth IRA account with the trustee that holds your traditional IRA and direct that trustee to move the money to the newly established Roth account.

2. *60-Day Rollover.* If you use this option, be careful and precise in the execution of the movement of these funds, as the current trustee will be making a distribution of your current traditional IRA, giving you 60 days to establish a Roth IRA account with a new trustee and effect the deposit of the distributed traditional account into the newly established Roth account. If you don't accomplish this in the 60 days allowed, the distributed amount, less any deductible contributions, will incur both federal and state (if applicable) income tax at your current tax rate, in the year you received it. To compound the problem, if you are under the age of 59½, you will also have to pay a 10% IRS early withdrawal penalty. (*For these reasons, we discourage this option.*)

3. *A Trustee-to-Trustee Transfer.* This tends to be the most common option. If done correctly, it eliminates the possibility of an unwanted distribution or having a penalty imposed. You simply instruct your current trustee, usually through a transfer request form, to transfer your traditional IRA to the new trustee of your Roth IRA account.

Remember that federal and state (if applicable) income tax will be assessed on the converted amount, less any non-deductible contributions made to your traditional IRA, taxed in the year of the conversion. You'll need to file and retain copies of the Internal Revenue Service Form 8606 to prove and verify the amount and year of all of your non-deductible IRA contributions in your traditional IRA.

When converting a traditional IRA to a Roth IRA that contains non-deductible contributions, you must use the pro rata rule that states the tax-exempt portion of your rollover must constitute only a pro rata share of the total rollover. An example would be having a $100,000 traditional IRA containing $40,000 of deductible contributions,

$20,000 of non-deductible contributions and $40,000 of investment earnings. The formula used to determine the tax exempt portion is the non-deductible contribution divided by the total value of the traditional IRA — $20,000 divided by $100,000 — qualifying you for 20% of the total amount transferred as tax exempt. So, if you converted $50,000 of the $100,000 total amount, then 20% or $10,000 of the $50,000 would be tax exempt. This rule is in place to keep someone from thinking they can convert only the non-deductible portion without having to pay any federal or state income tax on the conversion.

Along with traditional IRAs, there are other accounts that can be converted to a Roth IRA. They include simplified employee pension (SEP) IRA plans, federal government 457(b) plans, and 403(b) plans for school and tax-exempt organizations.

Even though conversions are taxable, you must remember that this tax is due in the future if you choose not to convert. The real question is: How advantaged or disadvantaged are you by paying the taxes due now? So we are back to the original question — to convert or not to convert? Let's look at some important factors that may influence the decision.

- **College financial aid** – If you have a child applying for financial aid for college in the year that you make a Roth conversion, it could make your income appear higher than it actually is on your income tax return. When your child completes the application, be sure to include supporting documents identifying the income anomaly as a conversion and not spendable income. Most financial aid administrators have the leeway to ignore such an anomaly.
- **Medicare Part B**. If you are covered by Medicare, the Roth IRA conversion can be problematic. Part B premiums are determined by income reported on your federal income tax return. A conversion to a Roth IRA would increase reported income and could cause your Part B premiums to increase for the following year.

If you do enough research and talk with different people, you will hear a host of different arguments, for and against, when it comes to the Roth IRA conversion. Let's looks at some of these.

- **You will pay a lower tax rate in retirement.** That may be true. If you know for sure that you will be in a lower tax bracket in retirement, then it would definitely be smarter to pay the taxes in retirement rather than convert to a Roth and pay the tax now. But you need to ask yourself this question, "Where will tax rates be in five years? 10 years? 25 years?" Many people feel that the decisions facing our country's leaders, as it relates to our national debt, may lead us into higher tax rates.
- **Your investments inside your traditional IRA are doing very well.** When the stock market enjoys bull market highs, this may be true for people. As a result, you must consider the fact that you pay ordinary income taxes on the converted amount in the year of the conversion. Many people have chosen to convert during down times in the market; the logic being that the taxable amount is lower, and the growth on a future rebound would be tax-free. My personal opinion is to not let recent account changes (positive or negative) factor too heavily into the Roth IRA conversion decision.

Many reasons expressed by traditional IRA owners and even so-called financial experts have almost a mythical explanation or sound to them explaining why you should not convert your traditional IRA to a Roth IRA.

For example, you should never convert your traditional IRA to a Roth if you have to pay the taxes out of the traditional IRA. No question, if you are going to pay the taxes from the traditional IRA, there are some roadblocks and issues you will want to be wary of. One of the biggest is if you are under age 59½, you will incur the 10% IRS penalty for early withdrawal. A little later, I will share a strategy to combat this issue for you would-be converters who are under age 59½. But for now, let's assume you are over age 59½ and the only way you can convert and pay the accompanying tax bill is from the traditional IRA you are converting. Let's pretend again that you convert $100,000 of a traditional IRA and use $28,000 of it to pay the taxes on the conversion (assuming, of course, a 28% tax bracket). If the remaining $72,000 is left to grow at an assumed 6% for 10 years, the value would be $128,941 — yours to spend without additional taxation. But let's continue and assume you don't convert the $100,000 from your traditional IRA and it grows at the same 6% rate of return over the same 10 years. It would grow to $179,084, ready to be taxed. If you are still in the 28% tax bracket, you would owe $50,143 in income tax on the $179,084 inside your traditional IRA, giving you $128,941 of spendable cash. This example does not illustrate state or local income tax on either scenario, but if the tax rates are the same, so is the outcome. So, it's an even push, but where is the advantage? The truth is that the Roth IRA provides some flexibilities that the traditional IRA did not.

The biggest advantage to the Roth IRA is that you can enjoy tax-free income withdrawals in retirement. This income has no effect and cannot increase the taxes due on your Social Security benefits. This may or may not impact you, but for many people this can be a significant tax reduction.

Also, with your traditional IRA, at age 70½, you will be forced to take (or penalized if you don't) required minimum distributions (RMDs), whether you need the income or not. Failure to take your RMDs results in a penalty of 50% of the minimum amount that should have been taken over the amount actually distributed.[1]

An additional benefit to the Roth IRA is for the next generation. Anything left to the next generation in a Roth account is passed on tax-free instead of taxed at their tax rate if they inherit a traditional IRA.

You are starting to see the pros and cons of the Roth IRA decision. As you think more about the decision to convert, you may hear somebody say, "You're close to or in retirement. It takes years for a conversion to pay off."

Let me say it again "plan first, *convert* second." Understanding where you are in regard to your tax bracket is really the key here. There isn't one universal right or wrong answer. This statement comes from the idea that the cost or tax paid to make the conversion from a traditional IRA to a Roth IRA may take years of tax-free growth to make up for the taxes paid. When you look at the example given earlier of a conversion of $100,000 in the 28% tax bracket, having a federal income tax bill of $28,000 sounds logical at face value.

But remember, as I mentioned earlier, someone is going to pay the tax bill of your traditional IRA — either you, in your lifetime, or your heirs after your death. It is kind of silly to think that in order for the conversion to be worthwhile, you have to make up the tax amount that is going to be due sometime in the future anyway. Unless the conversion puts you into a higher tax bracket, it is pretty much break-even financially from the first day. However, starting with day two, you are financially ahead for the simple fact that tax-free earnings are always better than tax-deferred earnings. But if the conversion does take you into a higher tax bracket, then what you would have owed on the traditional IRA, it would take time for the tax-free earnings to overcome the additional cost.

After a few more examples, I will give you some strategies to help keep you in a favorable tax bracket when converting.

I hear this quite often, sometimes as a statement and sometimes as a question, "After you convert your traditional IRA to a Roth IRA, your money is not available for five years." Whether statement or question, you need to understand the rules for withdrawing money from a Roth before you attempt to do so. The Roth IRA, including conversions from a traditional IRA, is one of the most flexible retirement accounts available. This flexibility is key.

Not everyone's life goes as planned. As you could imagine, I am a big advocate of retirement planning and retirement savings. Over the years,

I have seen many people who are financially successful and are big savers in 401(k)s, IRAs and other tax-sheltered investment vehicles, have a life-altering event that forces them to liquidate those investments. As a result, they end up paying income tax and penalties on this distribution, causing an erosion of capital amounting by as much as one-third to one-half of the total account value.

Roth accounts offer a little more flexibility through the understanding of what are qualified and non-qualified distributions. How are distributions from a Roth IRA taxed? According to the Internal Revenue Service Publication 590, when a distribution is made from a Roth account, the IRS assumes that the first money withdrawn is from regular contributions made to the account. If the withdrawal is larger than the contribution amount, the IRS then assumes it is coming out of conversions or rollovers made to the account. And if the withdrawal is more than the contributed amount, the converted amount and rollover amount, the IRS assumes that the balance taken is from the earnings inside the account.

Let's look at an example of a Roth distribution and how taxes and penalties might apply.

Meet Tom

Tom is 49 years old and has been working at his current job for four years. He has a 401(k) plan worth approximately $75,000 and is vested 50% in the contributions made by his employer. He has a traditional IRA from a rollover from a previous employer worth $250,000 and a Roth account worth $275,000 that contains $75,000 worth of contributions, $125,000 converted from his traditional IRA four years earlier and $75,000 from the earnings of the investments. Tom has had an unforeseen financial issue arise that has put him into a position of needing $100,000 additional cash. His bank is only willing to loan him $25,000 and would require him to pay it back, plus interest, within 12 months. The $100,000 needed is over and above the $100,000 emergency fund he has. Tom was in the 28% federal tax bracket and 6% state tax bracket. What are the options for putting together the cash?

The $25,000 bank loan is not enough, and he is concerned with having enough extra income to pay it back in the year required. He hasn't been at his current job long enough to qualify for a loan from his 401(k) or be eligible for an in-service distribution. He has a traditional IRA rollover from his previous employer, but he would lose almost half in taxes and penalties (28% federal income tax, 6% state income tax and 10% early withdrawal penalty), requiring an almost $200,000 distribution to try and net the $100,000 that he needs. But what about the Roth account? If Tom takes $75,000 (remember the order of the distribution assumed by the IRS) from the Roth account, that is considered to be from his contributions.

As a general rule, you can withdraw your Roth contributions at any time without paying a tax or penalty, and it's considered a qualified distribution. Tom needs $25,000 more. The next withdrawal comes from his conversion four years earlier. If he takes the $25,000 from the converted amount now (a non-qualified distribution), he would pay no income tax because he paid it at the time of conversion and instead would incur a 10% penalty on the $25,000 for not following the five-year rule (more on the five-year rule in a moment). In summary, the penalty cost to use the Roth account would be approximately $2,500 rather than the (nearly) $100,000 it would have cost him out of the traditional IRA. But wait a minute, what if Tom used the $25,000 bank loan for one year — getting the conversion past the five-year rule, allowing a qualified withdrawal to pay off the bank loan not incurring income tax or a penalty? That could be another consideration for Tom.

The lesson learned here is that the Roth IRA offers more flexibility with distributions and planning. I am not recommending that you use your Roth account as an ATM, but you can certainly get some tax diversification through proper use. Remember, a qualified distribution from a Roth IRA would be both tax- and penalty-free and a non-qualified distribution may trigger both taxes and early withdrawal penalties.

Let's talk about that five-year rule, as this can make Roth withdrawals a little more complicated. To understand the five-year rule, we need to go back to withdrawals from traditional IRAs. If you take a withdrawal from a traditional IRA before age 59½, any part of the distribution that is taxable is also subject to a 10% penalty (there are a few exceptions).[2] Taxing authorities had a fear that people would use Roth conversions to avoid the penalty rule on a traditional IRA. Instead of taking money directly from a traditional IRA and paying a penalty, convert it to a Roth and pay the tax. Then make a distribution from the converted amount in the Roth — paying no income tax, thus circumventing the penalty since no tax was due and the rule states that the penalty is imposed on the taxed amount. To keep this from happening and to close this loophole, a special rule was imposed — the five-year rule. If you take a distribution from the conversion money in a Roth account within five years of the conversion, the early distribution penalty will apply even though the distribution was not taxed.

There is a lot of misinformation out there surrounding Roth IRA conversions. In fact, every once in a while I'll hear somebody say, "A Roth IRA conversion is irreversible." There could be some good reasons why a conversion may look or sound good at the time of conversion but look completely different a few months later.

Let's look at an example. You want to convert a traditional IRA with a value of $30,000 to a Roth IRA. From the conversion, you would owe income tax at your current tax rate for the year of conversion. Let's assume that the investments inside that IRA performed very poorly, and by the end of the year, the value of the converted Roth fell to $15,000. Would you feel good about paying the income tax on $30,000 now that you only have $15,000? Probably not. The good news is that you can re-characterize your converted Roth account back to the traditional account and not pay taxes on the conversion, as long as you do this before October 15 of the year after the conversion. This is like a tax do-over. Who would have thought?

One of the best reasons I have heard to not convert to a Roth is giving your IRA to charity. Charities don't pay income tax. Why would you pay the income tax and then give a tax-free Roth to an institution that will pay no tax on the full amount of the traditional IRA?

This chapter has been all about exploring the positives and negatives of the Roth IRA conversion. Let's look at a few more positive reasons why you might want to consider converting.

- **You have additional money outside the traditional IRA to pay the income tax due when converting to a Roth account.** When you use money from an account outside the traditional IRA, it is the equivalent to making a contribution to the new Roth account. Pretend that you have a traditional IRA worth $200,000 that you would like to convert to a Roth account, and you also have a savings account with $50,000. You are also in the 25% income tax bracket. The $200,000 traditional IRA after taxes would be worth $150,000. By paying the tax on the conversion with the savings account, the $200,000 traditional IRA becomes a $200,000 Roth IRA. This is the equivalent of a $50,000 contribution to the Roth account. Remember, a normal contribution has much lower limits. This can be a great opportunity to add a significant amount to a Roth account. If you had invested the $50,000 into a regular investment account, you would have to pay taxes on all the earnings. By adding this money into the Roth account, all of the earnings will grow and compound tax-free through the payment of the tax. An added bonus is that in five years after the conversion, you can withdraw (for any reason) the entire converted amount of $200,000 without having to pay any tax or penalty. You do need to remember that any earnings made on the $200,000 conversion are still taxed and would have an early withdrawal penalty if taken before age 59½.
- **A Roth conversion can also make sense if you want to avoid required minimum distributions (RMDs).** Traditional IRAs

and other retirement accounts that hold pre-tax money force you to take RMDs. Roth accounts are not subject to RMDs, allowing your money to grow income tax free for a longer period. A good strategy for this might be to wait until retirement when you are in a lower tax bracket. After looking at your personal situation and the future need for the traditional IRAs that you have, you'll see some advantages in your situation in converting to a Roth account (plan first, convert second). You also want to employ some strategies when making the conversion.

Many laws and rules surrounding a conversion to a Roth account, coupled with your individual circumstances, can aid in developing a strategy for conversion, for example, the rule that allows you a do-over as late as October 15 of the year after the conversion. Here is a way to hedge your conversion. Let's say you were to make a $150,000 conversion from a traditional IRA. Let's also say the traditional IRA is currently invested in three different investments you are happy with, you want to continue using these same three investments in the converted Roth account, and you have money in your savings account to pay the tax on the conversion. Instead of opening one Roth account for $150,000 and using three investments in the one account, consider opening three Roth accounts with $50,000 invested in each one of the three investments as a tax hedge. You do need to be aware that each Roth account may likely have a separate IRA maintenance fee (usually $50 per year or less).

What's to gain by doing this? After you have made the conversion, one of the three investments, for whatever reason, has lost money and the amount of tax you owe is for a larger amount than the investment is currently worth. You would have the ability to re-characterize the Roth account with the loss, preventing paying taxes on the loss but still giving you the ability to keep the two accounts that have grown tax-free. If you had made the conversion to only one account, you are faced with having to pay the tax on the loss in order to reap the benefit of the gains in the other two accounts. Using this strategy gives you the ability to pick and choose which Roth conversion accounts to keep and which to re-characterize back to a traditional IRA. The accounts kept can then be consolidated into one account, eliminating the extra maintenance cost. The cost of the extra Roth accounts should be considered like an insurance premium, a small amount to pay for protecting what could be an uncomfortable amount of unneeded taxation. Remember, this needs to be done by October 15 of the year after conversion.

Another strategy that comes from recognizing an opportunity and understanding the rules and laws and applying them to your own situation would be a person under the age of 59½ who would like to convert a traditional IRA or retirement account to a Roth but does not have enough money outside of that account to pay the taxes on the conversion. If they were to use the money from the traditional IRA, that would be subject to the 10% early withdrawal penalty due to them being under 59½. This person could use Rule 72T, allowing substantially equal payments from their traditional IRA. It's called a parceled withdrawal system based on your life expectancy. As the payments are received, you can use them to systematically convert the payments from the traditional IRA to a Roth account. The payments are taxable, the same as making a normal conversion, but you would avoid the 10% early withdrawal penalty. It is worth mentioning that if you are 70½ and are taking RMDs, you cannot convert those payments to a Roth account.

The one conversion strategy that I encourage all retirees to consider, but I still advise the "plan first, convert second" philosophy, is using what might be the lowest tax bracket you'll be in for the rest of your life by using a series of smaller conversions. Remember the story in chapter 5 about the farmer? Would you like to pay income tax on the seed you were about to plant or on the whole harvest when it comes in? Of course the amount of tax on the seed would be much less than the tax due on the harvest. It would be silly to pay the tax on the harvest.

In a sense, that is exactly what we have done with our traditional retirement accounts. We either take a tax deduction when contributing to an IRA, or contribute pre-tax dollars to a traditional retirement account. When you reach retirement and want to use that money for income, it's harvest time and one of your largest assets has an unknown tax future. Would you be more comfortable paying a tax rate that you are familiar with? Consider this strategy in retirement. Around June or July, run what I call a "dummy" tax return. You would have six months of actual income data leaving only six months to estimate your income for the year, for the purpose of determining where you are in regard to how much more income you could have without going into the next tax bracket. For example, if you are in the 15% tax bracket and you could have $15,000 more income before going into the next tax bracket, would it make sense to systematically convert this amount at what may be the lowest amount of tax paid and do this every year? It may take several years to convert a meaningful amount to a Roth account, but this ultimately gives you a tax-free income and growth option by slowly paying some of the tax now. The tax-free nature of the Roth IRA may give you a little more confidence later in retirement if the government decides to bump tax rates.

These are just a few of the strategies and ideas that are possible using a Roth conversion in conjunction with your overall financial plan. To be truly able to answer the question to convert or not to convert can only be answered through proper planning and coordination. Remember, *plan first and invest second,* and *plan first, convert second.* And anytime you hear blanket statements made about finances and taxes, you owe it to yourself to take a look under the blanket.

Chapter 7

Social Security Maximization — What Every Retiree Ought to Consider

By Christopher Tanke

The driving principle behind my firm can be expressed in just four simple words: **Plan Smart, Retire Smart**. Because of this, we spend a great deal of time helping people transition from the accumulation years (work) into their distribution years (retirement). There are many issues retirees will have to solve for as they plan for their retirement futures including how to create sustainable retirement income from their nest egg, market risk mitigation, minimizing taxes, rising health care costs, wise inheritance strategies, and more. *The key to long-term planning is to look at the client's financial picture holistically, and then coordinate assets in such a way to work together to provide the income needed in retirement.*

As you can imagine, having assisted hundreds of families in their retirement transitions over the years, we've learned a thing or two about best practices for retirement planning. With this background in mind, I'd like to give you a significant piece of advice that you really need to take to heart. Are you ready? Here it is . . .

The manner in which you decide to take your Social Security benefit is one of the most important financial decisions you will ever make.

Your decision:
- on average will account for 30-40% of your retirement income.[1]
- could have a significant effect upon your spouse's well-being when you're gone.

- if made incorrectly, could mean the loss of a lot of money that you could have received from the Social Security Administration (SSA) over your lifetime but didn't.
- is revocable within the first 12 months. If you feel you've made a mistake within the first 12 months, you may withdraw your application and pay back your benefits.[2]

My purpose of writing this chapter is simply this: You've been paying into SSA all of your life. I think you deserve to know how to make the most out of your investment! With an introduction like that, you're probably thinking, *"Of course I want to maximize my benefit, but where do I begin?"* Well, let's start by taking you right to the source, the Social Security Administration website at ssa.gov. There you'll find many useful articles on Social Security; but I suggest we begin with one of their white papers, "When to Start Receiving Retirement Benefits." [3]

Once you open the report, let me encourage you to carefully read the first two paragraphs of it. There are two important takeaways embedded within these paragraphs that you cannot afford to miss.

"You should make an informed decision about when to apply for benefits based on your individual and family circumstances."

"We hope you'll weigh all the facts carefully and consider your own circumstances before making the important decision about when to begin receiving Social Security benefits."

This advice cannot be understated. In our experience, the hasty decision to begin benefits as soon as possible is the root cause of all Social Security mistakes and missed opportunities. Yield not to temptation!

In the end, when it comes to savvy Social Security strategies knowledge is key. Therefore, to coach you along toward your optimal election, I've arranged into two parts what I believe you need to know at a minimum:

Social Security 101 – Understanding Basic Claiming Strategies

Social Security 201 – Understanding Advanced Claiming Strategies

The following information is based upon 2017 Social Security rules and regulations, which, as we all know, is subject to change.

Let's begin!

Social Security 101 – Understanding Basic Claiming Strategies

Get It Right the First Time

Your Social Security record represents a lifetime of significant contribution on your part (paycheck and income deductions) through Federal Insurance Contributions Act (FICA) taxes. In fact, it's quite possible that you have invested more of your hard-earned money into your Social Security record than into your company 401(k) or IRAs. For this reason, we encourage our clients to manage their Social Security records and options with as much care as they would their own retirement accounts and investments. This is a revolutionary concept for many, but it shouldn't be.

If you're like most retirees, you will probably be supplementing your Social Security checks with funds from your nest egg. Imagine that your annual Social Security benefit is $30,000 but you want to live on $60,000 in retirement. How much would you need to amass in your retirement accounts to create an additional, predictable $30,000 a year to go along with your Social Security checks? That number may surprise you. If you follow the historical 4% rule (never take more than 4% out of your accounts in any given retirement year[4]), you would need to have approximately $750,000 in your investment accounts to create $30,000 a year. That's not an insignificant sum. The truth is, you may need to start treating your Social Security record with a lot more respect! There is tremendous value wrapped up in your record and that value needs to be maximized.

Action point: Think of your Social Security record as an investment to be managed, more than an income stream to elect.

Make Sure You Qualify for Benefits

If you have a light or sporadic work history, you may or may not qualify for Social Security benefits. To be eligible, you must have earned at least 40 credits to qualify You earn these credits when you work and pay Social Security taxes, and it depends on the year you were born. If you were born in 1929 or later, you need 40 credits (10 years of work).[5] In 2016, you would have received one credit whenever you earned at least $1,260 from a job in which FICA taxes were paid.[6] The maximum number of credits that can be awarded in a year is four. For example, if you earned $5,040 in January and February and then hit the beach for the rest of the year, you will still receive your maximum four credits for that calendar year ($5,040/$1,260 = 4 credits). Keep in mind that these 40 credits do not need to be gathered in succession, so if you have been in and out of the work force over the years, you may still easily qualify. You must be at least 62 years of age to start taking Social Security. Spousal, divorce and survivor benefits will be discussed later.

Action point: Go to the Social Security Administration website (ssa. gov) to review your record to make sure that you qualify for benefits.

Verify Your Earning History

This is a big one. When calculating your benefit, the SSA looks at your highest 35 earning years and combines them in such a way as to create what they call your average indexed monthly earnings (AIME). It is important that you review your earning history with the SSA to confirm that the data they have on file for you is accurate. If you have missing years or under-reported years, this will certainly affect your AIME number, which in turn will affect your primary insurance amount (PIA). Your PIA is the benefit you would receive if you elected it at your full retirement age (FRA). By the way, this explains why, in general, a person with only 10 earning years will receive a lesser benefit than a person who worked 40 years. With 10 working years, the SSA will add in 25 zero-earning years and solve for your AIME based on 35 total years. With this in mind, you may find it valuable to work a few more years and replace some of those zeros!

Action point: Go to the Social Security website to review and confirm your earning history.

Understanding the Math Behind Your Options

It's been said that timing is everything. This is certainly true when it comes to the size of your monthly Social Security check! Understanding your options begins by identifying your FRA. Find your year of birth and its corresponding age on this chart:

Your Year of Birth	Full (Normal) Retirement Age
1943-1954	66
1955	66 and 2 months
1956	66 and 4 months
1957	66 and 6 months
1958	66 and 8 months
1959	66 and 10 months
1960 and later	67

Source: Social Security Administration

Remember your AIME number? That number is used as the basis for calculating your PIA at your FRA. For every full year you elect to start benefits before your FRA, you'll receive an approximate 6.6% reduction; for every year you wait to receive your benefit after FRA, you'll receive an 8% simple-interest raise. Based on the chart above, let's assume that your FRA is 66 and your PIA benefit at that time is $2,000 a month. If you elect to receive your benefit at age 62, you'll receive a monthly benefit of $1,500. If your FRA is over 66, the reduction will be greater.[7] However, if you wait until you're 70 to start, you'll receive a monthly benefit of $2,640. Some would make the case that by delaying taking benefits, one could participate in an attractive, government-backed guaranteed rate of return. While this may be true, it is certainly not the whole story, as you will see next.

Action point: Go to the Social Security website to find your PIA at your FRA.

Can You Live with Your Break-Even Point?

Let's assume once again that your FRA benefit is worth $2,000 a month. Let's also assume that you have just retired at age 62 and after much thought have decided to hold off starting benefits until you reach 66, in order to receive a greater monthly amount. That could be a very good decision on your part, especially if you are in good health and have longevity in your family. However, make no mistake, you just voluntarily gave up receiving $18,000 a year for four years (starting at age 62 you could have collected $1,500 a month).

In other words, by the time you start receiving your first monthly $2,000 check at age 66, you could have already deposited $72,000 into your account. So when do you get all that money back? In most cases, we find the break-even point to be around 80 years of age when it comes to cumulative benefits. Therefore, if you decided to wait until after age 62 to start receiving your benefits and don't live to age 80 then you would have not broken even.

Action point: Buy a juicer and start jogging … Live Long and Prosper!

Always Consider "Opportunity Costs"

Your election is not made in a vacuum. In fact, in almost every case, the way you decide to take Social Security will have immediate impact on a variety of financial issues such as your income tax liability, whether or not your spouse can start a spousal benefit, how much you're allowed to earn in semi-retirement, and more often than not, the amount of money you'll be compelled to withdraw from your retirement savings.

Back to our break-even point for a moment. If you decide to forgo taking the $18,000 a year from age 62 through age 65 for the opportunity to receive $24,000 a year beginning at age 66, do you think you will miss any of that money in the meantime? If "yes," you may, out of necessity, be forced to withdraw $18,000 per year out of your retirement savings each year to make ends meet until you reach 66 ($18,000 x 4 = $72,000). What would $72,000 have grown to by the time you reach 80 if you hadn't withdrawn it from your savings to fund your deferred Social Security strategy? That is a very important question that must be calculated into your overall retirement plan.

Action point: Find a financial planner who can guide you through your election options holistically.

Get a Grip on Spousal Benefits

If you're currently married, you may qualify to receive a spousal benefit from your husband's/wife's Social Security record. If you have your own work record, then you have the opportunity to choose either. There are many combinations of ages, benefit amounts and other circumstances that must be taken into account when applying for this benefit. Eligibility rules also vary.[8] It can often be difficult to understand the effect your filing age can have. The Social Security website has more information, and below is only a summary.

1. You cannot elect a spousal benefit before the age of 62.[9]
2. You cannot begin your spousal benefit until your husband/wife begins their own Social Security benefit first. Maybe they are already receiving benefits before you apply. In any case, you can apply online or in person. Social Security will check your eligibility.[10]
3. If your spouse is not already receiving benefits, he or she can apply online for benefits based on age.[11]

Action point: Start talking together as a couple now about how you might coordinate spousal benefits within your overall retirement plan. Check the sources noted and do your research before applying.[12]

If Divorced, Know What You Are Entitled To

If things don't work out with your spouse, you may be entitled to elect a spousal benefit based on his or her Social Security benefit.[13][14] To qualify, it is important that you understanding the following:

1. Your marriage must have lasted at least 10 years. If you divorce prior to the 10-year minimum, that would mean no benefit for you.
2. If your ex-spouse has not applied for benefits but can qualify and is at least age 62, you can start receiving benefits if you have been divorced for at least two years.
3. Unlike spousal benefits, you do not need to wait for your ex to file for his/her own benefit before you can file on their record. However, you both need to be at least 62 years of age to begin receiving benefits.
4. As with spousal benefits, the maximum amount of ex-spouse benefit that you might receive is 50% of your ex-spouse's PIA amount. To receive this amount, you'll have to wait until your FRA before you start.
5. If you fall in love a second time, he/she better be worth it! Spousal benefits on your ex stop the day you get remarried.
6. Multiple ex-spouses can file for benefits on the same individual so long as they have been married to him/her for at least 10 years.

Action point: March down to the Social Security office nearest you and find out what benefits might be available to you. You'll need to bring your divorce certificate and your ex-spouse's Social Security number with you.

Understanding Survivor Benefits

If you are married, survivor benefits are going to play a part in your spouse's future. It's just the way the game of life is played. Here's what you need to know about your future options:

1. Except in the case of an accident, you need to have been married at least nine months to the decedent before you'd be eligible for survivor benefits.

2. If you are both receiving Social Security checks at the time that one of you passes away, the survivor will give up the lower benefit and assume the higher benefit. A person cannot collect on two Social Security claims at the same time.

3. Survivor benefits may start as early as age 60.[15] If you have a work record, you may start with a survivor benefit now and switch over to your benefit at a later time. This would allow your benefit to increase while you wait.

4. Unlike ex-spouse benefits which cease upon remarriage, if you remarry while receiving a survivor benefit you will have the option of either continuing your decedent benefit or switching to a spousal benefit based upon your new mate's record.

Action point: Survivor benefits can be tricky to maximize. It would be wise to discuss your options with a financial planner who is well-versed in Social Security options.

Watch Out for Your Earnings Test

This is one test that you cannot afford to fail! Did you know that you can work a job and receive Social Security benefits at the same time? It's true, but you must keep an eye on the earning test limits (ETL) while doing so. If you are under full retirement age, working and receiving benefits, the SSA will start reducing your monthly check if you make too much on the job and violate the ETL. For 2016, the sliding scale for earning tests was applied in this manner[16]:

1. If you make more than $15,720 on the job while taking Social Security between the ages of 62 and 64, the SSA will deduct $1 from every $2 you make over that limit.

2. If you make more than $41,880 on the job while taking Social Security at 65, the SSA will deduct $1 from every $3 you make over that limit.

3. Starting at your FRA, the ETL is no longer in effect!

What if you retire mid-year and want to immediately start receiving

Social Security but have already met your ETL for the year? Not to worry, the SSA has you covered with a special rule that allows you to receive your entire monthly check once you have officially retired, even if you have already reached your earning limits for the year. Here's how it works: Say you retire on September 30 at age 62. You want to start Social Security immediately but have already earned at work $60,000 for the year. In this case, the SSA would consider you retired on October 1 and not count the $60,000 against your ETL for that year.

However, for the remainder of the year they will divide your $15,720 in annual earning limits by 12 ($1,310) and then apply this monthly pro-rata earning limit to the remaining three months of this first transitional year. So if you work part-time in October, November and December, make sure that you didn't make more than $1,310 in any of those three months, and you'll receive your full Social Security check. By the way, most people think that when the SSA starts taking back benefits because of earning limits being breached that those dollars are lost forever. That is not the case. Dollars deducted from your Social Security check amount will be added back into your Social Security record when you reach your full retirement age. Because there are no earning limits at that time, you'll see an increase in your monthly check.

Action point: Your life will be so much easier if you stay away from earning limit violations each year. Keep track of what you are making and stay within the limits while receiving benefits between age 62-65.

Social Security 201 — Understanding Advanced Claiming Strategies

We are retirement income strategists who are fluent in a variety of advanced Social Security strategies geared toward maximizing our clients' benefits. I'd like to share two of our more popular approaches.

The "Hey Brother, It's Not About You" Approach

We are significantly outliving previous generations. If you're a male and in relatively good health, average life expectancy tables will give you a "shelf life" of approximately 83 years. Not bad! However, if you're married, your wife will probably make it to age 89. On average, women typically outlive men by six years.[17] Think about that for a moment. Suppose you married a woman five years your junior. We now know that if we go by average, she could be on her own for 11 years after you're gone. In this scenario, we already know exactly what is going to happen with her Social Security benefit. She is going to lose the lower benefit and keep the higher benefit for the rest of her life. (Remember, one person cannot receive a benefit on two Social Security claims at the same time.) If the husband was the higher wage earner, perhaps he should consider delaying starting his benefit so that his spouse will ultimately have a larger monthly check to live on later.

Action point: As the old saying goes by British scholar Thomas Fuller, "He that plants trees loves others beside himself." Your spouse may be in a much better long-term situation if you were to delay starting your Social Security benefits.

The "Restricted Application" Approach

This strategy could be valuable for both married couples and divorced individuals, so long as each party has qualified for benefits on their own. A restricted application allows a person to begin receiving a spousal benefit only, thus waiting to trigger their own benefit at a later date. This serves to put Social Security benefits into your pocket now while allowing your record to grow at 8% per year until you claim benefits on your own record. Allow me to illustrate:

Sally's PIA at 66 is $1,000

Sam's PIA at 66 is $2,000

Sally decided to start Social Security at age 62 and received a permanently reduced benefit amount of $750 a month.

Subsequently, Sam, upon reaching his full retirement age of 66, files a restricted application and begins receiving a spousal benefit of $500 a month (50% of Sally's full PIA).

Sam then initiates his Social Security benefit from his own record at age 70 and receives $2,640 a month (his benefit increased as a result of delayed retirement credits).

The takeaway is that if you wanted to wait to receive a higher benefit on your record later, why wouldn't you start receiving money before then on a spousal benefit if it was available to you? The SSA doesn't care if you file a restricted application or not, but isn't it a no-brainer to do so? At least that's what my kids would say about it.

Remember, to be eligible to execute this strategy:

1. You must be full retirement age or older and have not received any Social Security benefits whatsoever before you initially file for a restricted application. This means that you cannot file for your benefit at 62 and then file a restricted application at full retirement age.
2. You must have a spouse who has already started receiving their own benefit (otherwise, no spousal benefit option for you).
3. NEWS FLASH - The Bipartisan Budget Act of 2015 has mandated that the option to file a restricted application is now only available to those who were born before January 2, 1954.[18] So, if you didn't turn age 62 by January 1, 2016, the bad news is that you're just too young to take advantage of a restricted application in the future. The good news is you're just too young!

Action point: Find out what your spousal benefit at age 66 would be worth if you used this strategy.

Parting Words of Wisdom

As a retired chaplain in the U.S. Air Force Reserves, I am very much a military history buff. In fact, I think that as a society we do ourselves a great disservice by not respecting the experiences of those who have preceded us or by listening to the wisdom they pass on to us. In the spirit of this, we have a wise quote from one of our nation's greatest war heroes displayed prominently on large easels in both of our offices. You can tell that we think a lot of the quote, because it's the first thing you'll see as you walk through our front door. It's attributed to the late General Dwight David Eisenhower, who as a leader and tactician brought WWII to a successful end. To say that General Eisenhower knew a thing or two about strategy, outcome-based-planning, and getting things done is a great understatement. Here's the General's advice that rings as true now as the day he first uttered it.

"Plans are nothing; planning is everything."

These six words are always in the back of my mind whenever a client places their faith in me.

Everyone has plans and dreams of a successful retirement. Unfortunately, not many engage in comprehensive financial planning to increase the odds of that successful retirement actually happening. It is my sincere hope that this chapter, and in fact this entire book, will serve to both enlighten and inspire you to consider working with a holistic retirement planning firm that can coach you in the essentials.

Get after it my friends, for in the end those who **Plan Smart, Retire Smart**.

Chapter 8

Keeping a Level Head

By Levi B. Edgecombe CFP, CLU, ChFC and
Don W. Coplin, CFP, CLU, ChFC

A person who wants to be successful in any life endeavor is wise if he or she incorporates into their game plan an approach that confronts the obstacles that are most likely to thwart their efforts. Years ago we started our careers in financial services as life insurance professionals and realized early on that the greatest threat to our success was our fear of rejection. This is true of many people who are in business and sales positions. They fail in sales because they don't address this inherent desire to be liked, which results in many would-be salesmen not making sales calls in order to eliminate the possibility of being rejected. Successful salespeople learn to embrace what others avoid — making calls. They confront this fear of rejection head-on.

Fear and Greed

Interestingly enough, these lessons we learned early on have helped decades later with the investment portfolios of our clients. The reason for this is simple. Fear is one of two emotions that can wreak havoc on an investment portfolio. The other is greed.

For over two decades, Dalbar, an independent financial service research firm, has been examining the returns that investors actually realize and the behaviors that produce those returns. In the 2014 Quantitative Analysis of Investor Behavior (QAIB) study, the average equity mutual fund investor underperformed the S&P 500 Index by more than 4% in 2013 over the most recent 20-year period.[1]

Think about that for a second.

The average investor who invested in equity mutual funds "enjoyed" a return of 5.02% compared to an average return of 9.22% during the same time frame in the S&P 500 Index.[2]

Here's the key to remember: We're not talking about a short period here. We're talking about 20 years.

The study lists several reasons for this underperformance but determined the biggest reason was due to investor psychological factors, primarily the influence of risk aversion (fear) and herd mentality (greed), which resulted all too often in them buying high and selling low. Some of the all-time great investors shed light on how they were able to produce superior investment results by resisting the negative impact of these two emotions.

Bernard Baruch lived in New York City and was a famous investor during the first half of the 20th century (even coaching Winston Churchill on his investments). When asked the secret to his investment success, he replied, "I made my money by selling too soon." This man had developed a successful approach to dealing with greed as he also opined, "Nobody ever lost money taking a profit."

John Templeton, founder of the highly successful Templeton Funds, once said, "To buy when others are despondently selling (fear) and to sell when others are avidly buying (greed) requires the greatest fortitude and pays the greatest and ultimate rewards."

Dollar Cost Averaging

In our firm, we try to implement strategies to deal with these emotional factors because we understand that the behavior of our clients can easily undermine their long-term success. For the beginning investor who hasn't yet accumulated wealth, our firm has long advocated using the dollar cost averaging approach, which encourages a beginning investor to commit to a systematic contribution (preferably monthly) to purchase equities.

Using this approach, we tell our clients that the ultimate goal is to accumulate as many shares as possible over a long investment period with the understanding that market downturns will be their ally in this process; it is during those times that a greater number of shares will be purchased. Our firm is involved in the 401(k) market, and it's encouraging to hear from participants during annual reviews that they are thrilled when markets are down as they were able to buy more shares.

Many of the plans we have taken over had low contribution rates because employees were afraid of market volatility. However, after our education process they realized that this same volatility was really an opportunity for share acquisition. ("You buy your straw hat in the winter time.") Once one has built a substantial capital base (all in the eye of the beholder), what strategies can be deployed to preserve one's accumulated capital? Are there approaches that accomplish this by factoring in the fear/greed reality?

Alternate Methodologies

Many clients have been driven out of the equity markets because of the two-year downturn experienced in 2001–2002 followed by the 2008 collapse. Some call the 10-year period from 2000–2010 "the lost decade" as many investors were fortunate if they broke even during this time frame. So, how does one develop a successful investment game plan given the volatility we have experienced in the 21st century world of financial markets?

The U.S. stock market from 1980–2000 was essentially a sustained upward growth curve, and investment advisors encouraged investors to buy and hold during this span of time. Investors were taught that temporary declines would soon be followed by greater advances, and they simply needed to weather the brief appearance of fear and stay the course with their portfolio. That approach did not produce attractive returns for the first 10 years of the 21st century. We suggest some alternative methodologies that we use with our clients to help them navigate these turbulent waters in order to preserve and grow their accumulated wealth.

Divide portfolio into three sectors

In developing portfolios for clients, we break their portfolio into many sectors contained within three main categories: 1) equities, 2) bonds, and 3) alternatives. The equities in our portfolios are managed by two different approaches. First, we use a formulaic trending system, which uses active management and quantitative mechanical methodologies and models to create strategies to match our clients' needs. The algorithms use a strict quantitative system and model for each strategy to determine on a regular basis what type of investments to buy and then ultimately how long to hold each one before selling. This trending system operates on the underlying premise that there are times when it is appropriate to be in the equity markets and times when one's funds should be parked either in a money market or bond fund until the scoring system deems it is time to once again participate in the equity market. Because there isn't any human emotion in this computer-generated system, these formulaic algorithms eliminate the emotions of fear and greed.

The second portion of equities held in our portfolios is called "satellites." Here, different styles of analysis are used to locate sectors and stocks that have the potential for nice returns. With fundamental analysis, we look for stocks with intrinsic value (what they are really worth). This determination of worth for the stock is the sum of its discounted cash flows.

Qualitative analysis

Another option we use is qualitative analysis, where we look at the management team of the company. We want to know who is running the company, why they are running it, and what their philosophy is. Another factor is what products and services they provide.

Technical analysis

The last option we use is technical analysis, also commonly called "charting." This type of analysis is the polar opposite of fundamental analysis. With this approach, multiple types of charts are used to determine what could be an appropriate fit for the satellite holdings.

When we purchase these positions, we do so using multiple techniques, such as trailing stop losses, limit orders and stop losses. These techniques are options to address both sides of the psychological continuum. By putting a limit on the loss, we are addressing the fear side of the equation, and by setting an acceptable top-side gain on when to sell the position, we are confronting the greed end of the continuum. We try to add return to our clients' portfolios by using equities, but doing so in such a way that will address the basic emotions that could derail our attempt at making market gains.

What's Wrong with Being Greedy?

Greed can be defined as an excessive desire to gain or get ahead. Some may say, "What is wrong with a desire for making big gains?" There is nothing wrong with proper analysis resulting in a substantial winner, where, for example, an investment in a blue chip company or a penny stock captures large gains. However, when one disregards the fundamentals of the holding and gets caught up in the emotions of chasing big returns, then greed becomes the out-of-control villain. Many times we see this happen when individuals get involved in a "get rich quick" scheme.

Sometimes being at the right place at the right moment will provide the unexpected bonus return, but in most cases, that is not the normal outcome. In fact, quite often when greed drives the decision-making and the desired outcomes don't materialize, then greed's brother FEAR commandeers center stage and often causes the strongest of individuals to make irrational decisions. This is why when we make a satellite purchase, we up-front set an acceptable profit so that we avoid falling prey to the "being a hog" mentality; yet with our trailing stop loss in play, we can ride the stock past this preset profit level knowing that once it starts to drop, our trailing stop loss will automatically sell the position and lock in the majority of the gain for our clients.

We've had several clients referred to us who have unfortunately been out of the equity markets since 2008, and they had avoided the market because of their painful experience that same year. Many individuals, because of buy-and-hold advice, stayed the course and rode the market all the way to the bottom in 2008 and the beginning of 2009. Some of these same investors were so fearful at the bottom that they weren't able to complete the hold part of the strategy and have been in cash ever since, compounding these losses since they provided themselves no chance for recovery. Even buy and hold would have been better than their selling low choice. The impact of fear on an investor can result in them losing just as much or more than the investor who is controlled by greed.

Which Should You Own?

We also have bonds in our portfolios, and just like the world of equities there are many different styles to choose from. The most common sectors are Treasuries, corporates, governments, convertibles, high-yields and floating rate funds. So the question always is, "Which should you own?" The answer will be different for everyone, and, ultimately, it depends on your goals.

If you are taking the dividends as long-term income each month, then you are not as concerned with the price and value of the bonds as long as you continue the income until maturity. If you are not taking income and simply own the bonds as a portion of your portfolio, many advisors take the same approach with bonds as they do with stocks … buy and hold.

Just as with our equity portfolios, we like to use trends to determine what types of bonds to own and when to own them. We track such indicators as Treasury rates, buying and selling pressure and credit.

We also track the share price of the bonds and factor in monthly and quarterly dividends to show overall return, which helps our clients get the big picture of the cumulative performance of their bond holdings. This system helps us minimize the emotions that normally erode most investor portfolios when share prices decline.

Additionally, bonds are added to the portfolio to add negative correlation. What this means is that when equities move in one direction, bonds often will move in the opposite direction. An investor never wants his entire portfolio to move in the same direction. Theoretically, it would be desirable to have the whole portfolio make gains every day, but if all of the holdings are correlated and another 2008 happens, then this entire correlated portfolio would also take a downward spiral.

At the same time that an investor has correlated and non-correlated holdings in a portfolio, investments with neutral correlation also need to be added. These holdings move independent of all the other investments and comprise the "alternatives" portion of our portfolio design. We use a correlation matrix generated by Morningstar to constantly audit all of the holdings (investments) within each of our portfolios to see if we have a good mix. If too many holdings are diverging from their normal correlation, then changes have to be made to bring the correlation back in line to also control risk, return and other factors. For neutral correlation, we like to use different types of investments such as commodities, non-traded real estate investment trusts (REITs) and private equity.

We implement these strategies with the hope of providing more balance to a portfolio, but there is no specific strategy that can guarantee a profit or prevent against a loss. Our hope is to help mitigate potential market volatility while still providing consistent returns for our clients.

Making Your Money Last Longer Than You

One of the most highly charged emotional times for our clients is when they make the decision to retire. They will no longer be receiving a paycheck and will embark on the longest vacation of their life — some lasting 20 to 30 years. Their greatest fear is that they will run out of money. So how do we deal with this reality?

We begin by helping our clients make wise claiming decisions for their Social Security benefits and developing a plan that coordinates all of their other income resources and financial assets to maximize the possibility of their assets lasting longer than they do. During this planning, one of the key risks we want to corral is the sequence of return risk that will confront their portfolio. Our inherited clients who had retired in 2008 and were told that they could safely withdraw 5% per year from their equity portfolio realized after a year of devastating loss that their plan was not going to work. They were the unfortunate beneficiaries of beginning their retirement years with a horrendous first year sequence of return.

How do we build a portfolio to address the potential of negative losses in the beginning years of one's retirement? First, we divide the portfolio into segments or what we would call "buckets." Each bucket is designed to have its own purpose in the financial plan and would also have an appropriate amount of risk assigned to it. (Chapter 4 also discusses buckets and provides examples.) By doing this, we are able to reduce the emotional impact of volatility. This approach has been a wonderful way for us to create an income distribution plan for those entering their retirement years. When the client knows that his initial bucket of income is from a lower risk fixed-income portfolio then he can relax — other buckets that will provide income in 10–15 years will be in equities but won't be touched for another 10–15 years. Knowing that his initial years of income are coming from a lower risk source provides greater probability that he will emotionally weather any volatility occurring in the longer term buckets. In years where there are substantial gains in the longer term growth bucket, we quite often use some of those profits to replenish the income bucket.

Once these buckets have been constructed, we ask our clients to treat their portfolio just like the guy who interrupted them this morning while they read their daily newspaper at the coffee shop ... forget about him. What we mean to say is, don't get personally attached to the individual holdings in your portfolio. Forget the name and the price of each of the holdings and focus on the total portfolio or bucket.

We preach this because very little of the market's volatility can be explained by changes in underlying fundamentals. Markets are volatile even in the best of times. Make sure that you stay invested for the term of the bucket. No matter if your bucket is 1–3 years or 15 or more years, invest for the full length of that time, however, make sure that you are constantly adjusting according to the market returns and your goals.

Risk Tolerance

In constructing the buckets mentioned above, our firm determines each investor's risk tolerance so that the investments can match their stated ability to take on risk. Each investor needs to look at their portfolio and determine the important issues in growing it for the future. First, be comfortable with the holdings in the portfolio. Again, if fear, greed and other emotions do not allow the investor to feel confident with their portfolio, then adjustments need to be made during semi-annual meetings. But make sure that the adjustments are based on substantial and well-established data.

Make sure the plans are on pace to meet all of the client's goals. If they are, then increasing the return to hoard more money by taking more risk might need to be discussed. If the plan and the return of the current portfolio is adequate, why take on such risk? Being able to tell your friends that your portfolio is growing at 15% a year might be impressive, but if all you need for your plan's success is 6% annually, then the additional risk and accompanying emotions should be carefully considered.

What's Considered a Loss?

Shooting for a greater return might enhance the portfolio, but what if it created a devastating loss? An investor has to determine what would be a devastating loss. Would a loss of 10% or $100,000 on a $1 million portfolio be a devastating loss or would it have to be 50% or $500,000 on the same portfolio? A loss of this magnitude might not seem as traumatic for a 35-year-old, but for a 65-year-old, it could possibly be a life-changer. As long as the risk of a portfolio is properly quantified and accepted up-front by the investor, then losses within this expected range for their risk tolerance are easier to weather in the heat of such a loss. We don't want the frustration of an "acceptable" loss to drive our clients out of the market.

Semi-Annual Reviews

All of the above advice sounds reasonable to us, but we have realized that unless it is reinforced on a regular basis through semi-annual reviews, then our clients are unlikely to follow through on the above strategies. We wholeheartedly believe in planning first and investing second. Our planning department understands that each client needs to create a plan and stick to it.

When markets are tough and volatile, clients can feel confident knowing that we have factored their desired budgetary categories into our planning projections and that they have been funded and updated on a regular basis. We know that providing semi-annual updates of their plan along with updated investment results helps maintain the equilibrium of their emotions. Just as the algorithms and tactical strategies are in place to control the emotions in the investment process, having in place an overall plan, which can include wills and trusts, is also a means to instill confidence in our clients. Create the plan, stick to the plan and monitor without frivolous adjustments driven by random noise emanating from the press.

Ignore the Media

Wow, what a world we live in. One day a small country wants to default on sovereign debt, the next, a dictator makes an irrational comment and the next, somebody accidentally turns off the power switch at a nuclear reactor and presto, the markets erupt. There is much volatility in the world markets today, so how does an investor make decisions on what to do with their portfolio? First, turn off the TV stock shows. CNN says the economy is great, and Fox says it's terrible. Stop listening to all of the noise on the airwaves. The emotional responses to these current events drives much of the volatility in the markets. Why else would we buy Apple stock today on the basis of qualitative analysis and expect to hold it for the next year to take advantage of all of the great new products that will be flooding the market, yet we sell it all tomorrow because a TV personality makes a negative comment? See, it is a two-edged sword ... our emotions cause market volatility and, at the same time, are influenced by the same market volatility. When we look at risk and how clients deal with risk, most references to risk itself are just references to emotions.

You Have to Be in It to Win It

If we look in the bible to the book of Matthew, chapter 25 and verses 14–30, we see "The Parable of the Talents." A very wealthy man called for three of his servants. He gave one five talents, the next two talents and the last servant one talent. A talent has been calculated to have weighed approximately 75 pounds, equal to about $1,200,000 of gold or the equivalent of 20 years of wages.[3] The wealthy man left for a long time, which could have been 5, 10 or 20 years, and then returned. When he discovered that the first two servants were stewards of his money (they had taken risks and doubled his wealth), he was very happy with them and praised them. The third servant feared losing the money entrusted to him and therefore hid it until the wealthy man returned. After taking the money back from him, the wealthy man rebuked him and cast him out. This story reinforces our contention that you have to be in it to win it, and if fear is controlling your investment decisions, then you are doomed for failure. Fear and his twin brother greed have to be accounted for in an investment plan in order to provide an investor a chance for success.

Philosopher Blaise Pascal once commented, "The heart has its reasons which reason knows nothing of," which can be appropriate in the realm of interpersonal relationships as intuitions and other leanings of the heart can often prove fruitful. However, in the realm of investing, allowing one's emotions to run unfettered often results in the same outcomes reflected in the Dalbar study – investors substantially underperforming the markets. Acknowledging the reality of the influence of emotional factors on investor performance, our firm has devoted much time, and will continue developing well-constructed approaches to dealing with the culprits of fear and greed with the goal of increasing the investment success of our clients.

Chapter 9

A S.M.A.R.T. Approach for Managing Risk in Your Portfolio

By Jim Yent, ChFC, and Teresa Yent, CLTC, ChFC

[PREFACE: Please note that this chapter does not discuss the topic of "smart beta." Although there has been a lot of marketing hype and exaggerated claims about the benefits of smart beta, innovative ways of creating investment products out of stock indices (equal weighted, sector weighted, fundamentally weighted, technically weighted indices) have been around for almost 20 years. You may wish to talk with a financial professional for a discussion on the myths, as well as potential benefits of investing in strategies that use more logical and intelligent methods of selecting securities.]

Many of society's basic beliefs contain mistruths and misperceptions. There is no "dark side of the moon," we definitely use "more than 10% of our brain" and 2,000 years before Columbus "discovered America," both philosophers and sailors knew that we did not live on a "flat earth." How do such errors become accepted as unquestionable truths? We can thank the media, whether it was the printed pages of history books and magazines or today's 24/7 onslaught of news video, podcasts and tweets. Once we see it in writing or hear it on the news, we tend to believe it.

Investors also fall victim to the same mistruths and misunderstandings. Dr. Harry Markowitz, the "father of Modern Portfolio Theory," won the Nobel Prize for his groundbreaking work in the 1950s on portfolio construction entitled "Portfolio Selection: Efficient Diversification of Investments." Markowitz taught investors the benefits of well-diversified and efficient portfolios, and his insights became the bedrock of the "buy-and-hold" strategies that have dominated investors' portfolios for the past 50+ years. Unfortunately, few took Markowitz's own words to heart when he wrote:

> "The process of selecting a portfolio may be divided into two stages. The *first stage* starts with observations and experience and ends with beliefs about the future performances of available securities. The *second stage* starts with the relevant beliefs about future performances and ends with the choices of the portfolio. **This paper is concerned with the second stage.**" (emphasis added)[1]

So contrary to everything you have read or possibly believe as an investor, all the benefits of Modern Portfolio Theory begin *after* we as investors and advisors form beliefs about the future performance of our potential investment options! Markowitz did not give us a "pass" and tell us to simply make diversified and efficient portfolios and everything would be OK. Instead, he made us 100% responsible for the *first stage* — we are responsible for our portfolio's performance.

Now the twin market crashes of the 2000s begin to make sense. The S&P 500 Index fell 48% during the tech bubble of 2000–2002 and then declined another 58% during the mortgage meltdown of 2007–2009. These bear markets made many investors throw up their hands in disgust and despair. They began to question the merits of Modern Portfolio Theory, diversification, or a buy-and-hold strategy. Investors who had advisors were particularly aggravated that:

- There had been no "what if" planning prior to these crashes on how to effectively manage risk when a severe market decline occurs.
- The losses that investors incurred in their portfolios changed either their retirement plans or their anticipated lifestyle in retirement.
- The primary advice that they were given during this period was to "hold on and ride it out." And worst of all, these severe multiyear crashes happened not once but twice in a 10-year span, the so-called lost decade.

But from Markowitz's perspective, diversification did not fail nor did Modern Portfolio Theory. *We failed* to do our first stage responsibility to form a belief about the future performance of securities. Now this can be hard medicine to swallow in an age where every financial disclosure we have ever read includes language warning us that "past performance is no guarantee of future performance" which, of course, is true. However, this doesn't excuse investors or advisors from having open minds and clear vision when using modern techniques to assess future performance of available investment strategies.

The key words are "open minds" and "clear vision," because to effectively use modern tools of risk management, an investor needs to overcome two major fallacies that are generally accepted as conventional wisdom.

Fallacy #1: Investors need to embrace the long-run time perspective of portfolio theory. Although this sounds like sage advice given to the average investor, it's likely not to happen. The problem isn't that Modern Portfolio Theory is not an accurate and useful tool for describing portfolio performance. It's that even institutional investors (of pension funds, insurance companies and college endowments) who plan on 3-year, 5-year, and decades-long time frames do not plan on the 40- to 70-year time horizon that portfolio theory embraces. In other words, no one's long term is long enough to match the time frame assumed by Modern Portfolio Theory.

Before you reject this statement, let's examine the facts. Cliff Asness, founder of AQR hedge funds and a pioneer in managing risk-balanced portfolios, provided the following analysis to help investors understand the difference between the textbook view of long-term risk/reward and what actually happens in the stock market.[2] For comparison purposes, his analysis annualizes monthly returns that are in excess of cash, as well as annualizing monthly volatility. The charts on the following pages are from his analysis. Chart 1 illustrates the typical 45-year time horizon from 1970–2014 used to explain the risk/return characteristics of three asset classes:

- U.S. Treasury bonds have the lowest returns and the least amount of volatility.
- The S&P 500 represents large-cap stocks that have high returns and high volatility.
- The S&P GSCI Commodity Index has historically had higher returns and volatility compared to bonds but lower returns and higher volatility compared to stocks.

Chart 1

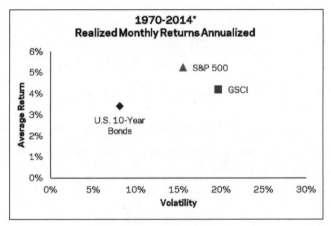

* Data for 2014 includes January through November

Chart 1 looks like it came right out of an Investing 101 textbook: Bonds earn a 2%–4% risk premium over cash, while large-cap stocks enjoy a similar 3%–4% risk premium over bonds for a 5%–8% premium over cash. Most investors would agree that five years is a "long" term perspective, so let's break this 45-year period down into nine successive five-year periods and see how often the five-year long-term risk/return matches the 45-year "longer" term view used by portfolio theory. The first five-year period (1970–1974, chart 2) instantly invalidates the 45-year expectations for risk and return. Stocks should outperform bonds, not underperform by 10%. Bonds are expected to earn a 2%–4% premium over cash and not yield a near-zero return, and commodities are not expected to deliver 25% excess returns.

Chart 2

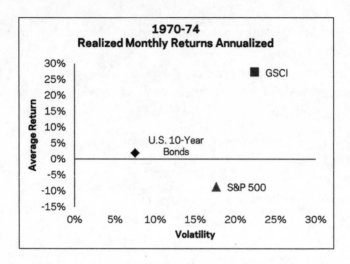

Chart 3 shows the 1975-1979 period and it doesn't look much better. Stocks have at least earned a positive return but have not recouped their losses over a 10-year period. Worse still, bonds deliver negative returns while commodities provide near-zero returns.

Chart 3

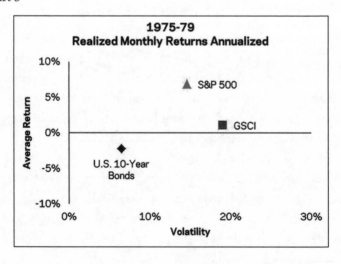

Chart 4 shows the 1980–1984 period and doesn't even receive a two-out-of-three ain't bad score — although stocks and bonds earned a positive but subpar return. Bonds did not deliver 3%–4% in excess of cash nor did stocks earn 3%–4% over bonds. Bonds were nearly as volatile as stocks were during the period. As for commodities, well, the long-term expectation wasn't to lose nearly 10%. Interestingly, this period suffered a severe recession. Yet stocks did not crash and bonds did not outperform as diversification and portfolio theory would predict.

Chart 4

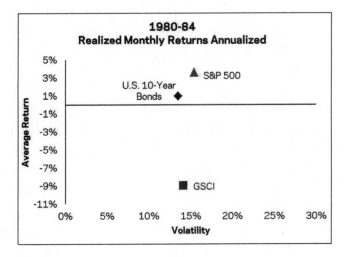

The 1985–1989 period is displayed in Chart 5. Hooray! We finally have risk/return results that resemble our 45-year longer term expectations. Stocks outperform commodities, which outperform bonds. The problem is the numbers are **too** good. It would be nice if bonds could earn 10% excess returns over cash and stocks would earn 12% premiums over cash — who wouldn't invest in the market with performance numbers like that! But the longer term 45-year perspective does not support such expectations. By the way, the stock market crash of 1987 occurred during this period, also called Black Monday, and was the Dow Jones Industrial Average's worst single-day loss ever of –22.6%.

Chart 5

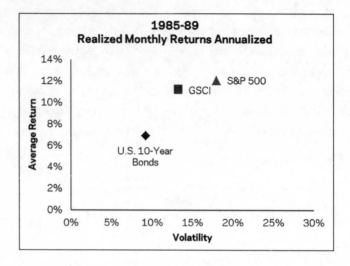

At the risk of oversimplifying things but with the intent of summarizing the conclusion that it's by now hopefully obvious, see the remaining five charts from Cliff's Perspective. Whether it's the boom years of the 1990s, the twin crashes of the lost decade of 2000–2010, or even the post-crash bull market that followed, the bottom line is clear: <u>Investors rarely experience the long(er) term risk/return behavior that portfolio theory is built upon</u>. As a result, investors need to do as Markowitz recommended: Do a first-stage assessment of how they believe the market will perform over the next few years and then allocate their investments accordingly.

Remaining Five Charts, also from Cliff's Perspective, of the 5-Year Performance

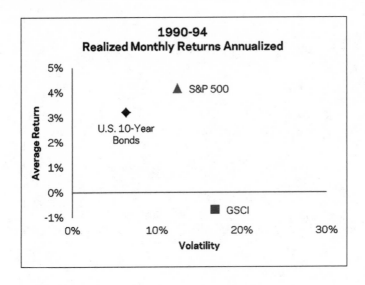

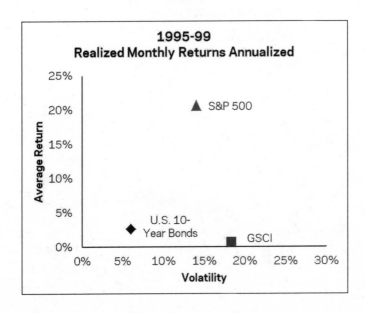

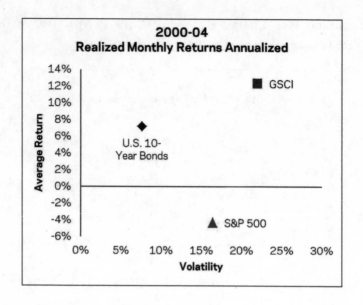

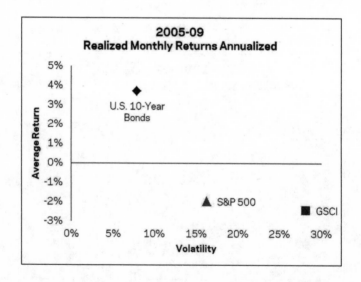

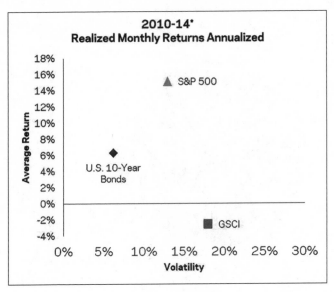

Before we discuss how to use modern techniques to manage risk in your portfolio, we need to clear the air on one more mistruth.

Fallacy #2: Ninety percent of all portfolio performance is driven by asset allocation rather than security selection or timing.

This is truly the whopper of all investing misinformation because a) the myth still persists today, and b) the investment industry and media do so little to correct this misunderstanding. Once again, let's return to the facts of how this urban legend was created. It all began with a 1986 landmark study conducted by Gary P. Brinson, Randolph Hood and Gilbert L. Beebower called "Determinants of Portfolio Performance." Brinson, Brian D. Singer, and Beebower published an update to the study in 1991. If you conduct an internet image search for "determinants of portfolio performance," you'll see numerous versions of chart 6 on the next page, which is Investopedia's version and explains that "The asset-allocation decision, otherwise known as investment policy, is arguably the most important determinant of a portfolio's long-term return."[3]

Chart 6

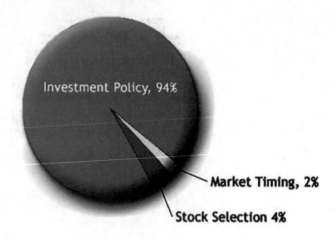

Investment Policy, 94%

Market Timing, 2%

Stock Selection 4%

Source: Investopedia

Even well-respected information sources (like Investopedia.com) continue to support the misunderstanding that the primary determinant of portfolio performance is asset allocation (Investment Policy).

Roger Ibbotson, founder of Morningstar's Ibbotson Associates and a finance professor at Yale's School of Management, described this "universal misunderstanding" of the Brinson studies as follows:

> "In fact, a survey by Nuttall & Nuttall (1998) demonstrates that out of 50 writers who quoted Brinson, only one quoted him correctly. Approximately 37 writers misinterpreted Brinson's work as an answer to the question, "What percent of total return **is explained** by asset allocation policy?" and five writers misconstrued the Brinson conclusion as an answer to the question, "What is the impact of choosing one asset allocation over another?" (emphasis added)[4]

What researchers have been trying to correct since the late 1990s is that the Brinson study communicated that over 90% of the *variability* of a portfolio is explained by asset allocation, not 90% of the performance. To drive this point home, Ibbotson later published several studies that tried to set the record straight. What he found was that 70% of the variability in portfolio performance was determined simply by the directions of the market — stocks or bonds in a rising or declining market. More startling, Ibbotson showed that asset allocation was equally as important as active management in explaining the variance of portfolio returns.[5]

Once again, investors need to heed Markowitz's advice: What are your expectations on how specific sectors or asset classes will perform in the future? Once an investor has an opinion about future returns, then they can use portfolio theory to allocate in a risk-managed way. In retrospect, it really was quite naïve to believe (or worse still, try to get other investors to believe) that all an investor has to do is have a good asset allocation strategy in place and they will be "fine." Perhaps more interesting is the wave of "robo-advisors" springing up — internet-based services that help guide an investor into creating a diversified asset allocated portfolio. Three phrases immediately come to mind for post 2000 investors:

- "Buyer beware."
- "You get what you pay for."
- "Fool me once, shame on you. Fool me twice, shame on me."

Once an investor clearly understands the two fallacies and their implications, the question comes to mind: How does an investor handle the ebb and flow of markets?

The answer is that investors need to be S.M.A.R.T.: **S**ystematic **M**anagement of **A**ssets using a **R**ules-based **T**echnique. Credit has to be given to Arun Muralidhar who coined this acronym when discussing portfolio rebalancing in his book, "A SMART Approach to Portfolio Management: An Innovative Paradigm for Managing Risk." Modern Portfolio Theory has always encouraged the practice of rebalancing your portfolio periodically, whether the rebalance was performed quarterly, semiannually or annually. Muralidhar described the issue perfectly when he said that the decision to rebalance or not to rebalance, the amount of changes an investor makes during a rebalance, in essence, any action or inaction that an investor or advisor makes to a portfolio is *active management*:

> "So, all asset managers must realize that every decision — whether to overweight, underweight, or to continue to allow assets to drift (not rebalance) — is an active decision, whether it is made explicitly or implicitly. In short, all these approaches are tactical in nature, even though they are not labeled as such and are often even cloaked as just the opposite!" [6]

When the undeniable logic of this statement hits you, it is difficult for an investor to not embrace a more active approach to risk management. S.M.A.R.T. portfolio management is a powerful tool for plotting a course, and more importantly, staying on course, to working toward your financial goals. Muralidhar asks the real-world question: Would you board a cruise ship headed to a distant remote island that merely sets "the rudder in the direction of the destination without adjusting for wind direction, tides, or choppy seas, and without considering potentially faster ways of reaching the destination with less risk of drowning?" If we are truthful with ourselves and we *knew* that was how the captain and crew were going to pilot that ship, few of us would board (let alone pay) to take such a journey. So why tolerate a naïve cross-your-fingers approach to our financial journeys?

Let's explore S.M.A.R.T. approaches to managing risk and return in your portfolio. S.M.A.R.T. is not a single technique but a toolbox of techniques that are applied to your portfolio. As the acronym implies, it is not subjective nor emotional — it is systematic. Every S.M.A.R.T. strategy has its own particular "secret sauce" on how it attempts the following:

- "Picking" investments by:
  - Asset class (stocks, bonds, alternatives, real estate)
  - Size (large-cap vs. mid- or small-cap)
  - Style (growth vs. value or core vs. satellite)
  - Sector (manufacturing, technology, health care)
  - Segment (investment grade, high yield, class floating rate)
  - Or geography (domestic, international, regional or country specific)
- And "protecting" your assets from downside risks through:
  - Proactive management
  - Reactive management
  - Event-based management

The secret sauce is the set of rules, algorithms or formulas that the strategy uses to pick and protect. As a result, S.M.A.R.T. strategies are often labeled as a technical or quantitative strategy because they have explicit rules on how and when it picks and protects. The rules are secret because many vendors will only partially disclose the techniques that they are using — the vendors often outline broad and general techniques that they are using so that advisors and investors can "peek under the hood" to see how the S.M.A.R.T. engine works. Rarely does a vendor provide the entire design "blueprints" so that a do-it-yourself (DIY) investor could build his or her own S.M.A.R.T. strategy.

If the vendor does disclose 100% of the algorithms, they usually do so because they know that they are the low-cost producer for that technique. In other words, although it is possible to recreate the strategy from the disclosures, it is cost prohibitive for individual investors to undertake such a project. The analogy to a home improvement project is helpful: Although many industrious DIYers will remodel a kitchen, bath, or other projects rather than hire a carpenter or plumber, DIYers rarely build their own houses from scratch. They clear and excavate the land, lay the footings and foundation, rough-in the plumbings, etc. As the size, scope or mission-critical nature of the project expands, even

DIYers call in the cavalry and hire professionals to get the job done. Returning to investment-management projects, this is particularly true of retirement and income efforts because investors, from a practical perspective, only have one chance of implementing their retirement income plan properly. Like other high-stakes activities, doctors don't operate on themselves or their family members. That's a pretty good rule of thumb for DIY investors, as well, when it comes to retirement income portfolios.

One of the common criticisms that is raised against S.M.A.R.T. portfolio management is that they use market timing. It is absolutely true that no one can successfully time the market. However, it is a misunderstanding to label S.M.A.R.T. strategies as "market timers" for several reasons:

- First of all, as Muralidhar explains, every investment decision has a timing aspect, even when you do or don't rebalance a portfolio's strategic buy-and-hold allocation.
- More importantly, as we will discuss in a moment, S.M.A.R.T. strategies agree that no one can time the market. Instead, they aim to trend the market in one of several methodologies. It is crucial to understand the difference between timing and trending.
- Finally, to be fair, no strategy works 100% of the time. For that matter, what in our daily lives besides death and taxes is 100% certain?

In the real world, many things are extremely useful and valuable that often have probabilities of success that are less than a 50/50 coin toss. Consider the butt of many jokes on inaccuracy: weather forecasting. Many of us would agree that weather forecasting can be incorrect: Is it going to rain or snow? Will it be two inches or a foot? Will the storm arrive tonight or tomorrow? The more precise we ask our weather forecasters to be, the more incorrect they are. But who among us decides to go to the beach when a storm is forecasted or doesn't grab a coat or umbrella when the forecast indicates that it would be prudent to do so.

So we have to be sensitive to the definition of "success." What batting percentage does a major league baseball player have to hit for the season to be considered a good hitter? Many would say a .300 hitter.[7] What shooting percentage does a 3-point shooter in professional basketball have to achieve to be considered a good shooter? The top 10% in the NBA shoot 38% or better.[8]

And when an investor actually does what he says he will do, the results become more dramatic. Let's exclude fanatical loyalty to one's college alma mater or their favorite pro team: Who wants to place a significant cash bet on a long shot? By significance, let's say 5%–10% of your net worth. And by a long shot, let's say the odds are somewhere between 5 to 1 and 10 to 1. Someone might place this bet, but the vast majority of investors would never do it.

Why? Because numbers count and math matters. The same is true for S.M.A.R.T. strategies that manage risk. If S.M.A.R.T. strategies can help lower your risk by even a small percentage, the effect that this will have on an investor's wealth is huge.

So how do S.M.A.R.T. strategies help an investor to minimize risk? All of these quantitative techniques use some form of trending (not timing) for picking and protecting a portfolio. In general, there are two approaches:

- Reactive or trend *following*, and
- Proactive or trend *forecasting*

All quantitative strategies make decisions based upon one or more fundamental or technical factors. These factors are analyzed to determine whether the factor's trend is improving or deteriorating. Examples of factors that are frequently used in S.M.A.R.T. strategies are:

- Fundamental factors:
  1. Beta or the risk premium of an asset relative to cash or a benchmark.
  2. Size or the premium that small stocks earn over large stocks.

3. Value or the premium that inexpensive assets earn over expensive assets.

4. Large groups of profitability (return on investment (ROI), earnings per share (EPS)).

- Technical factors that mathematically describe price movements over time:
  1. Momentum indications — moving averages, relative strength indicators and various oscillators.
  2. Chart patterns.

Trend *following* strategies monitor one or more factors and then take predetermined actions when factors cross a threshold or trigger an event. Trend following strategies act much like a thermostat in your home, constantly monitoring the temperature factor and either turning on the heat if the temperature drops too low, or turning on the air conditioning if the temperature gets too warm. In this manner, these strategies are reactive — when a factor changes from a desirable state to an undesirable state, the strategy begins to make adjustments. By definition, a trend following strategy will never buy at the lowest price or sell at the highest price — the goal of *timing* the market. Instead, these reactive strategies will identify a trend *after* it has occurred and then take action such as buy, sell, reallocate or even go to cash. Trending is very different from timing.

In contrast, trend forecasting strategies use pattern-matching algorithms to compare current factor trends with historical trends. When a match is found for current market conditions, trend forecasting strategies analyze how the market performed over the next "X" days in past cases. These techniques then calculate probabilities for how the current market may perform over the next "X" days. Many of these strategies adopt a "win by not losing" or "smooth the ride" approach to their adjustments by not reallocating into assets that have high probabilities of large gains or losses. These S.M.A.R.T.

strategies prefer to pick assets that have a high probability of a small gain and a low probability of a small loss. Given that this is a forward-looking perspective, these strategies attempt to be proactive — they have the ability to make adjustments before a triggering event occurs based upon probabilities of how the asset performed during similar past situations.

Regardless of whether discussing trend *following* or trend *forecasting* methods, the average investor has been told repeatedly that factor-based techniques are "useless," "not effective" or statistically "insignificant." Many investors believe that only one factor, "beta," or the market risk premium, has been definitively proven to be the repeatable and statistically significant predictor of portfolio performance. In portfolio theory jargon, this is called the Capital Asset Pricing Model (CAPM). Stated in plain English: If you want a better return, then you have to take more risk or beta.

Like the dark side of the moon or a flat world theory — the Main Street understanding of portfolio performance is flawed. S.M.A.R.T. factors have been accepted by academics and practitioners alike as meaningful tools to enhance not only portfolio performance, but far more importantly, to create portfolios that deliver superior risk-adjusted performance.

Eugene Fama and Kenneth French share the 2013 Nobel Prize for their publication on "The Capital Asset Pricing Model (CAPM): Theory and Evidence."[9] Fama and French convincingly demonstrated that there were two additional factors that significantly drove portfolio performance in addition to beta or the risk premium. Fama and French added a size factor and a value factor — the second and third factor in our list of fundamental factors discussed earlier. Their theory became so well-known and accepted within the investment community that it became known as the Fama-French three-actor model (FFM). All three factors were shown to be instrumental in determining portfolio performance.

In 2014, Fama and French extended their model to five factors and added a profitability factor and a conservative factor to their mix.[10] In addition, French and many academics have published significant research substantiating the predictive power of several other factors including a momentum factor and a liquidity factor.[11]

If the FFM has been public knowledge for over a decade, and these Nobel laureates and other thought leaders from both academia and the finance industry are espousing five or more factors that help manage portfolio performance, why isn't the average investor aware of these developments? Surely it is *not* from an inability to understand or a lack of desire to learn. People interested in investments tend to be smarter, more educated and more motivated than the average American. So the absence of information on this subject is as puzzling as it is suspicious.

After all, what are the implications to the investor and the advisory community given that these factors matter? There are many, but one message rings out as clear as a church bell on Sunday: Both investors and advisors have to do more work than what they have been doing for the past 50 years. Specifically, they have to do Markowitz's first stage analysis of future market performance so that they can identify and then allocate funds based upon fundamental and technical factors that indicate favorable and more attractive investment outcomes. If this extra work is not done by someone, then investors should expect to continue to ride the market roller coaster — both up and down as market conditions shift.

Who gains from keeping the average investor in the dark? Certainly not the investor. The studies have shown that these factors meaningfully add to portfolio performance. Consider the following table, chart 7, published by Kenneth French:

Chart 7

Summary of Index Performance by Decade	1930s	1940s	1950s	1960s	1970s	1980s	1990s	2000s	1930-Present
CAGR									
French High Momentum	2.3%	12.9%	23.3%	14.1%	10.3%	18.6%	23.1%	0.6%	13.1%
French Value	-5.8%	17.2%	22.3%	10.7%	12.3%	20.4%	14.3%	4.0%	11.6%
French Growth	1.6%	7.4%	17.5%	8.0%	3.4%	15.8%	20.0%	-1.3%	8.9%
S&P 500	-0.5%	9.0%	19.3%	7.8%	5.9%	17.6%	18.2%	-0.9%	9.4%
Sharpe Ratio									
French High Momentum	0.21	0.73	1.49	0.71	0.29	0.53	1.13	-0.05	0.55
French Value	0.15	0.88	1.23	0.51	0.38	0.75	0.73	0.16	0.41
French Growth	0.19	0.53	1.27	0.35	-0.08	0.42	0.98	-0.17	0.36
S&P 500	0.15	0.59	1.38	0.35	0.04	0.54	0.96	-0.15	0.37

Source: RBC Capital Markets Research, Dr. Kenneth R. French

As the table indicates, the momentum and value factors are significant. As we said earlier (and will touch upon again), no factor or S.M.A.R.T. strategy will work 100% of the time — there are periods of underperformance and over performance. But in general, whether viewed in 10-year increments or taken over the long(er) 80-year time frame of French's study, these factors add 2%–3% to a portfolio performance. But by far, the most important finding for investors is that the value factor was 10% more effective (.41 vs. .37) and the momentum factor was more than 48% more effective (.55 vs. .37) on a risk-adjusted basis than a passive index-based buy-and-hold strategy. What investor does not want to receive a 10%–50% better risk-adjusted return? Increasing portfolio return by several percent is impressive, but delivering double-digit gains in risk efficiency at the same time *is* more value for an investor's dollar. In the end, risk efficiency is the secret of wealth accumulation.

So if investors are not being informed about S.M.A.R.T. factor-based strategies, who gains from investors' lack of information? Unfortunately, the obvious answer is the mutual fund companies and advisory firms who want the status quo. If firms can keep your wealth as is, then they can continue to receive fees while doing the least amount of work.

Hopefully, S.M.A.R.T. strategies don't sound too good to be true because they definitely are not. S.M.A.R.T. strategies require a lot of time, effort, knowledge and skill. Investors and advisors alike need to understand what they can and cannot accomplish with these techniques. For example, S.M.A.R.T. strategies proved to be very effective in minimizing losses during both the 48% tech bubble crash and the 58% mortgage meltdown crash. Depending upon which S.M.A.R.T. strategy an investor selected, losses during these periods ranged from single digits to the mid-teens — a significant reduction in risk! There was no magic in how they accomplished this feat. As we have pointed out, S.M.A.R.T. strategies are *designed* to identify trends and take appropriate action. A crash is one of the most obvious trends that can be identified. The twin crashes of 2000s are clear and sustained for not days or weeks but months and quarters. See charts 8 and 9:

Chart 8: Tech Bubble – April 7, 2000-November 5, 2002

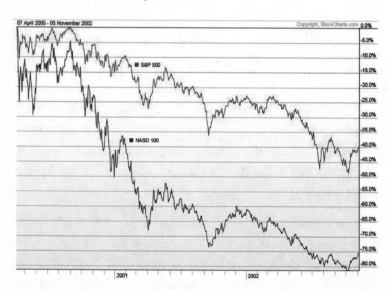

Source: StockCharts.com

Chart 9: Mortgage Meltdown – October 9, 2007-April 22, 2009

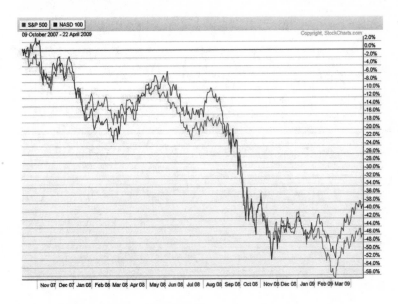

Yes, it is impossible to time the precise beginning or end of these crashes, but identifying and adjusting to these clear trends was not difficult for S.M.A.R.T. strategies. Only a die-hard buy-and-hold investor refused to play defense within the portfolio during the months and quarters that the market kept declining. No, the weakness of S.M.A.R.T. strategies is not during crashes or bear markets; the weak spot is when there is **no trend**. Consider the most difficult time period for S.M.A.R.T. strategies, calendar year 2011. Chart 10 is literally an image of a roller coaster: January 1 is where you get on and December 30 is where you get off. There were 14 separate reversals of 5% or more (a mini correction) in the market over the next 12 months — clearly there was no trend that lasted for more than a few weeks at a time.

Chart 10 – December 31, 2010-December 30, 2011

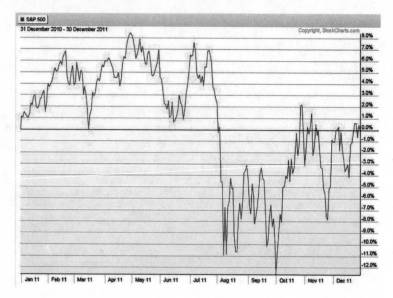

Source: StockCharts.com

In these trendless environments, S.M.A.R.T. strategies can get whipsawed by reacting to the change in trend just in time for the trend to reverse again. From what we have studied, trend following strategies whose threshold triggers were more sensitive to change and set "too tight" had a very difficult time in 2011 with losses in the high single digits to low teens. Trend following strategies, as well as trend forecasting strategies, whose triggers were set looser, did significantly better but still suffered small single-digit losses while the S&P 500 Index was essentially flat for the year.

S.M.A.R.T. strategies, as you can see, are not too good to be true. They can also break down and suffer losses or underperform a market under certain conditions. But when applied intelligently and diligently, they can provide a significant benefit to many portfolios.

Two final concerns are often raised about S.M.A.R.T. strategies: Are they tax efficient and are S.M.A.R.T. strategies diversified? Any strategy that trades for any reason other than tax harvesting will be tax inefficient. What can be more efficient than sitting on a stock for years at a time and never paying any taxes? Every investor wants to minimize taxes. As a result, many investors primarily use S.M.A.R.T. strategies in their IRA and Roth accounts. But not all S.M.A.R.T. strategies are created alike. Although some strategies definitely have high turnover ratios and are consequently tax inefficient, there are other S.M.A.R.T. strategies that have much lower turnover ratios, often in the range of some of the largest and most popular actively managed equity mutual funds. So a fair assessment is that an efficient S.M.A.R.T. strategy is about as "inefficient" as many of the mutual fund holdings in your 401(k) or IRA.

But discussions on tax efficiency might seem unimportant but can quickly become relevant. There has to be a discussion on the tradeoff between tax efficiency versus loss minimization. Without a doubt, all S.M.A.R.T. strategies will be tax inefficient when compared to an index exchange-traded fund (ETF) or a passive mutual fund. But if given a choice, many investors prefer to pay the tax rather than take a loss by staying invested in an index when it is plunging. This is particularly true when comparing long-term capital gains tax rates versus the loss potential of a bear market. The best approach for an investor is to think through or do a "what if" on these tradeoffs before a market decline occurs. An investor can then make an informed decision on tax efficiency versus minimizing losses.

The second concern is: Are S.M.A.R.T. strategies diversified?

Frankly, from a conventional perspective, no they are not diversified in the traditional sense. Often, conventional wisdom is that a diversified portfolio owns a little bit of many asset classes. S.M.A.R.T. strategies tend to be more focused in asset classes, styles, sectors, segments and geographies that are currently attractive on a fundamental or technical basis. Conventional diversification would own and continue to hold an asset even if it is unattractive. Yes, all investments are eventually "mean-reverting" — if they are unattractive now they will eventually become attractive again. But it can take a considerable amount of time before this cycle completes. Many asset classes have "boom or bust" cycles where stocks, real estate, oil, and gold can experience multiple years of high growth or abysmal performance. Traditional diversification encourages investors to place bets on both attractive and unattractive assets.

This leads us to our final realization about S.M.A.R.T. strategies: Investor views on diversification need to evolve. For years, investors have witnessed a slow progression of what the industry considers a diversified portfolio. In chart 11, state-of-the-art diversification has improved in one single dimension over the years by simply adding more types and more granular asset classes to create a diversified portfolio:

Chart 11

Investors have used multiple asset classes to address volatility

Evolving Diversification Strategies — A Historical Perspective

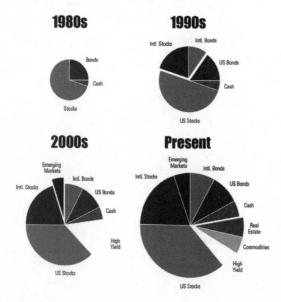

Source: AssetMark

Now is the time for diversification to expand from one single dimension — adding asset classes — to a multidimensional view on diversification. The primary lesson of the twin crashes of the 2000s was that traditional diversification was not enough. Investors still experienced large losses that meaningfully impacted their lives. Investors need to diversify across other dimensions to meet not only their wealth accumulation goals but to safely meet their retirement income needs. S.M.A.R.T. strategies are the building blocks for multidimensional diversification.

We recommend that investors consider the following four-dimensional (4D) diversification approach:

1) Current state-of-the-art techniques (e.g., a robust set of asset classes as shown in the "present" pie chart in chart 11 but with the following added levels of diversification.

2) _Diversify by purpose_ – Investors treat their money differently depending upon how they plan to use the funds. During our employment years, we earmark money for a variety of purposes: to pay bills, to save up for big purchases, for savings in our 401(k)/ IRA/Roth accounts, for future weddings and educational expenses, just to name a few. In retirement, these priorities shift to income replacement purposes: income for the first decade of retirement, required minimum distribution (RMDs) from your retirement accounts, income for retirement lifestyle goals like extra vacation travel, funds for potential long-term care and retirement health care expenses, gifts for children and grandchildren, etc. When investors give specific purpose for segments or sub-portfolios of their nest egg and then distribute these funds into specific accounts by purpose, these accounts can be managed far more effectively to ensure the funds are available to meet that need. The (lazy) alternative is to treat your funds as one big pot of money and try to manage it to accomplish these conflicting priorities.

3) _Diversify by time_ – This goes hand-in-hand with our previous discussion on "purpose." Money needed next year for a large

discretionary purchase should be invested differently from the funds you will use as a retirement paycheck or the RMDs that you receive 10 years from now. Time diversification allows an investor to create holding periods for accounts that are invested in more volatile assets like stocks. Once again, "Investing 101" teaches that the longer the holding period, the less variable are the expected returns of that (sub)portfolio. By creating a series of accounts with different and unique holding periods (e.g., a 5-year, 10-year and longer term sub-portfolio), an investor can smooth their own investment experience.

4) *Diversify by risk-management technique* – This chapter has hopefully introduced you to S.M.A.R.T. strategies that can provide much better downside protection than a traditional stock/bond/alternative portfolio. But just as most homeowners not only have a lock on their front door, they often also have a second deadbolt lock. And when you are in a big city hotel room, many people slide an additional chain or bolt lock. Why do we use multiple locks? Because if one locks fails, then hopefully the second or third lock might provide the security that is desired. The same principle applies to managing risk in an investor's portfolio. By all means, use S.M.A.R.T. strategies, but multiple "safety mechanisms" are better than one.

Managing a portfolio with S.M.A.R.T. strategies and four-dimensional diversification may be a new subject for many individual investors, but institutional investors (pension funds and college endowments) have been using these techniques for decades. The "smart" institutional money manager may have been managing portfolios often described as liability-driven investing (LDI) or a dedicated portfolio technique. At the risk of oversimplifying, LDI maps out the current and future cash flow needs (income and expense) that will be withdrawn from a portfolio. Isn't the sole purpose of a pension fund to be able to pay current retirees their pension checks for the rest of their lives and build a sufficient portfolio that will comfortably pay future retirees as well? The main focus of these plans is to put diversification constraints such as purpose, time and risk-management strategy on the aggregate portfolio. Individual investors could significantly improve their investment experience if they began to use similar techniques as institutional investors.

The message is simple: LET'S BE S.M.A.R.T.!

Chapter 10

Understanding Risk and Your True Risk Tolerance

By Drew Kellerman

In this chapter, we will explore the concept of risk, your tolerance for risk and the important role these have in your financial life. I know what you are thinking … *"BORING."* Please stick with me, though. I will strive to bring this to you in a way that is not only compelling and interesting, but arms you with critical knowledge to help you get the most from your money.

What Is "Risk"?

"Risk" is a small word with a variety of meanings. Merriam-Webster's dictionary offers several definitions, including:
- Possibility of loss or injury
- Someone or something that creates or suggests a hazard
- The chance that an investment will lose value

A simple way to think of risk is, "The possibility that something bad or unpleasant will happen." Upon reflection, it seems that every aspect of life — every decision or action — carries with it some degree of risk. If you ponder your own experiences, you'll probably agree that life itself is a continuum of calculated risks. You cannot live completely risk-free, because no outcome is truly 100% guaranteed. There are only *degrees* of risk that fall along a spectrum from low to high.

Reward: The Other Side of the Equation

Is that revelation depressing? Fortunately, there is more to this story. Risk is but one side of the equation. The other side is called "reward."

This is the benefit or payoff of taking a risk. One of life's maxims states, "The higher the risk, the greater the potential reward." The opposite is equally true. The lower the exposure to risk, the lesser the potential reward. This is known as the "risk-reward ratio."

We all understand intuitively that some of life's more thrilling and meaningful experiences will entail a higher degree of risk, but the potential rewards justify the risk. For example, do you enjoy skiing, hiking, biking or kayaking? Each of these outdoor activities is immensely popular, even though all of them pose a higher risk of accidents than lying in bed watching TV. So, why take the risk? Because these activities provide a number of "rewards."

Managing the Risk-Reward Equation

If the risk-reward equation permeates every choice in life, how do we make good decisions? We use our rational mind and accumulated knowledge to evaluate the potential risks and compare that to possible rewards. We calculate the probability that something bad will happen and balance that against the potential payoff. If the probability of a bad outcome outweighs the reward, we avoid it.

This is fairly instinctive when the risk-reward ratio is at an extreme end of the spectrum. For example, no one in their right mind would choose to swim in a river full of African crocodiles or attempt to fly an airplane without flight instruction. These levels of risk exposure border on suicidal, because the *probability* that something really bad will occur is nearing 100%. Very few possible rewards can justify this level of risk.

When it comes to your money, excessive risk exposure — a *very* high likelihood of losing some or all of your money — can also be relatively easy to spot and avoid.

For example, have you ever been approached by someone who wanted you to invest lots of money in their "million-dollar" business idea? This person usually has no business experience, no business plan, no track record of success in anything, and a long history of squandering money. No thanks!

Or, perhaps you have seen "investment opportunities" promising that you would double your money every year, or were guaranteeing that you would earn a high rate of return (i.e., 20% per year)? How would you respond? You would quickly dismiss these as fraudulent scams (hopefully). Experience and common sense has taught you that there is a very high probability you will never see your money again. The risks simply outweigh the potential rewards.

Risk Mitigation and Risk Elimination

Enjoying a meaningful life will involve taking some risks. That said, we can (and do) take steps to lessen our exposure to the most serious consequences should something bad happen as a result. Hopefully, all of us wear seatbelts when riding in a car and wear a helmet when riding a bicycle or motorcycle. These are examples of mitigating risk. Mitigating risk means taking reasonable steps to reduce our exposure to the more severe outcomes should the worst occur.

But here is the catch. Mitigating risk usually always involves a tradeoff. Taking precautionary steps often diminishes the enjoyment of the experience. The key is to ensure that the tradeoff is reasonable and balanced. This tradeoff can be described as incurring a cost or paying a price in exchange for the protection we desire. It applies directly to your financial life.

Wouldn't it be great if we could completely eliminate all financial risks? Of course, but that is not possible. As with other areas of life, attempts to completely avoid losses from one risk will create exposure to other risks.

For example, some people are afraid that a future liquidity crisis will cause the banks to freeze deposits and not allow them to access their savings. They watched the banking crises in both Cyprus and Greece, and are determined not to let that happen to them.

So, they literally put their entire savings into physical cash and keep it in their home. Risk avoided and problem solved, right?

Yes, sort of. What about the risk of theft? Or, fire? Not to mention the fact that now their money has no chance to grow, exposing them to inflation risk. (That said, it might be a good idea to keep some emergency cash on hand in the event of a natural or manmade disaster.)

Here is another example. Some Americans are convinced that the U.S. dollar is on the verge of collapse (and has been ever since former president Richard Nixon took us off the gold standard in 1971).[1] So, they have put all their savings into gold, silver and other precious metals. This attempt to eliminate one risk — currency risk — has exposed them to two others: market risk and asset allocation risk.

While gold is a form of savings, the U.S. dollar price of precious metals can fluctuate wildly, especially in the short term. What if they bought gold coins at $1,500 an ounce and now need to sell some of them to raise cash to pay bills? As of this writing, gold is trading for about $1,283 an ounce.[2] Selling now means taking a loss of $217 per ounce!

And what if the price of precious metals happens to remain flat — or drop — throughout their retirement? If this occurs, having all their eggs in one, precious metals "asset basket" could result in subpar investment growth, negatively affecting their desired lifestyle when they start drawing retirement income. (That said, it may not be a bad idea to own *some* precious metals as a "chaos hedge.")

These are extreme examples of how completely eliminating one risk leads to new risks. But what about a more common example of this phenomenon? Let us look at a hypothetical scenario that illustrates what millions of Americans have done with their portfolios in recent years.

Picture yourself on a beautiful spring day in 2012. You are too distracted to notice the pleasant weather, though. You are *way* stressed out. Why?

You are reviewing your retirement savings accounts.

Your nest egg was hammered with losses — twice! — in less than 10 years (2000–2002 and 2008), and 2011 was a gut-wrenching, volatile ride in stocks that ended with zero gains.

You have had *enough* of the stock market. You want to completely eliminate stock market risk from your portfolio, so you put all your money where it will be safe: in bonds and/or bond funds. After all, you would like to retire at *some* point!

Have you eliminated stock market risk from your portfolio? Yes. However, did you know that this protective move to "safety" potentially exposes you to three new risks that could have a big impact on your financial life and retirement plans? These are inflation risk, interest rate risk and default risk. (We will return to these risks later in the chapter.)

What Is Risk Tolerance?

Our risk tolerance — or comfort level with the possibility of a loss or injury — is highly individualized and appears based on two main factors: our perception of how risky something is and how much we value what is at risk.

Because of our emotional nature, it is critical that we determine, respect and factor in our personal risk tolerance. Knowing your true risk tolerance can potentially ensure that you never put yourself in the position of reaching your emotional breaking point.

What does risk tolerance actually mean in the context of money and investing? Well, think for a moment about your tolerance level with other things. What happens when you reach the limit of that tolerance, or your breaking point? Usually, we react emotionally even when we know we should respond rationally.

Here's a question you can ask yourself to help determine your true risk tolerance:

Over the next six months, what is the maximum loss I am willing to accept with my investments before I capitulate and sell at a loss?

When you think of maximum loss, think in terms of actual dollars, not just a percentage loss. For example, a 20% loss from a $1,000,000 nest egg means $200,000 of your money is now gone. Focusing on the dollar amount you could lose will help you to better gauge how you might react emotionally if that were to happen.

Once you arrive at a maximum dollar amount that you are willing to lose (i.e., *I don't think I could handle any more than a $40,000 loss over the next six months*), it tells you how much "volatility" you can tolerate. When you combine this knowledge with the appropriate time horizon for each of your accounts, you have a framework for building a nest egg portfolio with an ideal balance of risk/reward.

Uncovering your true risk tolerance is very important because emotional reactions usually do not serve us well with money and investing. In fact, emotional decision-making is precisely why so many investors eagerly buy when the market is nearing its peak, and then sell in disgust and despondency right about at the bottom of a market cycle.

We know the key to success in investing is to buy low and sell high, but that is much easier said than done. It requires a logical, rational approach to your money at all times.

Value

Our risk tolerance is greatly influenced by how much value we place on the thing that is at risk of loss. Placing your *life* at imminent and immediate risk usually brings heightened clarity. Most of us greatly value our lives (supported by our survival instinct), so our tolerance of potentially life-ending risk is very low. Conversely, the less value we place on something, the more tolerant we usually are of the odds that something bad will happen to it.

Interestingly, some people I consult with on their retirement planning are singularly focused on aggressive growth opportunities. They appear to have a high tolerance of market risk (i.e., losses of 20% or more) with their life's savings right as they are about to stop working. Are they not aware of the impact this could have on their future lifestyle? Do they not properly value this asset?

Let us focus on what you value with regard to planning for your retirement. What are your most valuable retirement resources? Which of your assets are your most precious? I'm asking you to think about it for a reason. Until you understand what you genuinely value, it is tough to have a meaningful conversation about something as abstract as risk.

As soon as you read "retirement resources," you might have pictured assets like savings accounts, investment portfolios, IRAs, 401(k)s, 403(b)s, 457 plans, Social Security benefits, pensions, rental property, etc.

What do all of these have in common? They are:

1. resources that can generate passive-income streams, or
2. contracts offering future, passive-income streams

Sure, some of these assets might be directed toward your heirs or to charity, but in most situations, they represent an income stream for you when you transition into retirement. In short, they represent cash flow or money.

Is it money that you value most? Many people are reluctant to admit that they place a great deal of value on money, for fear of appearing shallow or materialistic. This reaction is understandable, but think about what your savings truly represents.

Your Most Valuable Assets

Virtually everything you enjoy being, doing and having requires three things: your time, health and energy. If you think about it, each of these "assets" is tremendously valuable because they are:

- limited
- tend to dwindle over the course of your lifetime
- are difficult (or literally impossible) to get back once lost or spent

You might not have thought about these assets in this way before, so let us expand on this concept.

Time: No matter how wealthy you may be, you have only 24 hours each day. You cannot get that back once it's gone, and, like every other living being your total time here on earth is finite.

Health: This is self-evident, but our quality of life is directly influenced by our health. The poorer our health, the fewer options we have to fully enjoy and experience life. And once lost, good health can be difficult or impossible to regain.

Energy: Have you ever been so physically, mentally or emotionally exhausted that, even though you had an entire day with no commitments, you could barely get out of bed? Unlike when we were kids, most of us only have so much life energy each day to do the things we want (or must) do. And, as we get older, the amount of energy we have usually declines.

That is why — no matter who you are and what else you might value — your **time**, **health** and **energy** are your most valuable assets. And, guess what? Your nest egg stores all of these.

The True Value of Your Nest Egg

If you are like most productive Americans approaching retirement, you have invested decades of your time, much of your physical, mental and emotional energy and sometimes even your health in your jobs or careers. (Health? Think stressful work environments and deadlines, fighting traffic, eating on the go, no time or energy for regular exercise, etc.)

TIME + HEALTH + ENERGY ⇨ SAVED MONEY

Most of the active income you received (i.e., wages you earned) in exchange for your investment of time, health and energy paid for your ongoing life expenses, of course. However, assuming you have retirement savings, you had the discipline to save and perhaps invest some of that money for your future (your nest egg). And this money is going to serve a very special purpose when you retire: passive income.

When you retire, your monthly living expenses do not disappear. In fact, they may even increase for a while if you have some bucket list items to accomplish (i.e., special trips, a unique experience, etc.). Your need for income will continue for the rest of your life, and your retirement assets will pay for your desired lifestyle.

But what does passive retirement income *really* do for you?

If you boil it down, passive income:
- frees your time
- conserves your life energy
- potentially allows you to improve or recover your health

Please ponder this for a moment.

SAVED MONEY ⇨ TIME + HEALTH + ENERGY

When I ask clients what they most look forward to in retirement, virtually all their answers can be summarized into these three:

- freedom to do the things I really like to do
- opportunity to get in shape, exercise more regularly and live with less stress
- energy to take on the hobbies and activities I love

No matter how varied their hobbies, interests, desires and goals are, they all share the same core requirements to be, do and have what they want: time, health and energy.

How about you? What are you most looking forward to? What will your time, health and life energy be required for?

- More involvement with the grandkids? (*Definitely* requires all three!)
- Four rounds of golf per week? (Same)
- Volunteering in your community? (Yup, all three.)
- Starting that business you've always dreamed about? (All three, and then some!)
- Tackling all those books you haven't had the time to read? (Self-evident)
- Can't wait to "live" in your garden? (Certainly requires time, energy and health)
- Going to travel the world, or explore North America in your RV? (Do you see a trend here?)

You see, the passive-income streams generated by your savings, investments and other retirement assets are going to pay for your living expenses, freeing your time, conserving your life energy, and potentially giving you back your health.

Perception

How we perceive risk is driven by our underlying belief system. These subconscious beliefs, often programmed early in life by high-impact experiences, lead to our dominant thoughts about and emotional reactions to a perceived danger.

One of the fascinating and quirky things about people is that sometimes what we *perceive* as safe is actually far riskier than what we perceive as dangerous and vice versa. For example, some people don't think twice about their daily rush-hour commute in their car, but they are terrified of flying on a commercial airliner. Which is actually safer?

The National Safety Council compiled an odds-of-dying table using data from 2008 and illustrated the relative risks of flying and driving safety. It calculated the odds of dying in a motor vehicle accident to be 1 in 98 for a lifetime. For air and space transport (including air taxis and private flights), the odds were 1 in 7,178 for a lifetime.[3]

The opposite of this also occurs, especially when it comes to money and investing. Often, I consult with people who express a low tolerance for the risk of loss, but their portfolio contains several investments that calibrate on the high end of the risk spectrum. This is so because they perceive these investments as safe and are thus very comfortable with owning them, even though they are actually exposed to a high probability of loss.

Sometimes our perception of a risk aligns with the actual, statistical likelihood of a bad outcome, but many times it does not. This phenomenon highlights the differences in how we each perceive risk.

Financial Risks in Retirement

The aspects of risk we just reviewed will all play a role in your retirement, including:

- creating a new risk by eliminating another
- the risk/reward ratio
- mitigating risk vs. eliminating risk
- the cost of risk mitigation
- the importance of perceived risk
- risk tolerance

In the world of finance and investments there are many types of risk. Here are the most common that could affect you, listed alphabetically:

Asset Allocation: Investing either too conservatively or too aggressively and not adequately diversifying assets to sustain your portfolio throughout market cycles.

Default: When a bond issuer (borrower) won't be able to return your principal at the end of the loan term, usually due to insolvency and/or bankruptcy.

Inflation: When the rising costs of living undermine your purchasing power over time.

Interest Rate: Fixed interest rate investments may not generate sufficient income in retirement, and/or will lose value should interest rates rise.

Market: Losing your invested wealth, either temporarily or permanently, because of a major market downturn.

Systemic: The risk of collapse of an entire financial system or entire market that negatively affects virtually all asset classes at the same time (i.e., the global financial meltdown in 2008).

In addition to these widespread financial risks, several other money-related risks appear only when you are in or nearing retirement. Some of these are intuitive, others, not so much:

Excessive Withdrawal: Withdrawing your assets too quickly, undermining your retirement plan.

Lifestyle: You may not have sufficient income to maintain your expected standard of living throughout retirement.

Long-Term Care Expense: Unexpected long-term care expenses consuming a large portion of your retirement assets.

Longevity: Outliving your wealth and income sources.

Personal Event: An unexpected change in family circumstances (divorce, death, adult children returning home, etc.) may derail your retirement plans.

Sequence of Returns: Receiving low or negative investment returns in the early years of withdrawing your retirement portfolio, thus increasing the potential of prematurely running out of money.

<u>Tax</u>: Rising tax rates and/or unforeseen tax consequences (i.e., due to poorly planned IRA distributions) can significantly hinder the growth of your portfolio and diminish your after-tax income.

Yikes! Who knew that so many financial pitfalls existed when you approach retirement? And this is not even a comprehensive list of risks, either. Fortunately, many (if not most) of these risks can be mitigated with comprehensive and thoughtful planning. That said, let us take a deeper look at some of these financial risks to illustrate how they can impact a financial plan in retirement.

Bonds and Inflation Risk

Let's start with inflation risk. Your money has lost an <u>average</u> of 3.18% of its purchasing power <u>every year</u> since 1913.[4] When we apply this inflation rate average to the last 30 years, we can calculate that it takes about $100 today to buy what $38 did in 1985.

Put differently, your money has lost over 62% of its ability to purchase things for you since *Back to the Future* hit the big screen and Mikhail Gorbachev came to power in the USSR.

What does this have to do with bonds? Let us return to our hypothetical scenario when, in May 2012, you invested your entire nest egg in 30-year Treasury bonds to avoid stock market risk. Today, you would be earning about 2.54% in annual interest until you sell them, or the bonds mature in 2042 (returning your principal). So, even before taxes, the interest you are earning is not keeping up with the long-term, average inflation rate.

Granted, inflation has been quite low or even negative in recent years. Inflation risk, however, applies to the long term. Should inflation return to its historical average, these bond yields may not be enough to preserve your future purchasing power.

Over the long term, this can dramatically impact your standard of living. Yes, but your principal is safe, right? Actually, that may depend on future interest rates.

Bonds and Interest Rate Risk

Let us look at a risk that many bondholders do not fully grasp: interest rate risk. The price of a bond — the amount you will get if you sell it — moves in the <u>inverse direction</u> of interest rates. When interest rates go down, bond prices generally rise.

Interest Rates ↓ = Bond Prices ↑

The opposite is also true. When interest rates rise, bond prices drop.

Interest Rates ↑ = Bond Prices ↓

Did you know that in May 2012 interest rates (as reflected by 10-year U.S. Treasury yields) hit their lowest level since 1790? That's not a typo, just to be clear. We experienced the lowest interest rates since George Washington was serving his first term as president of the newly formed USA.[5]

Furthermore, the long-term price movement of interest rates is cyclical. Measured in decades, interest rates trend up for a while, then reverse course and trend down for a while. The last time interest rates hit a multi-decade low was 1945. Interest rates then reversed course and trended up until 1981.[6] That is a 36-year interest rate uptrend, which is a *long* bear market for bonds!

Now, we are 34 years into an interest rate downtrend, meaning bond prices have generally gone up for a long time. Bond investors have enjoyed what amounts to a three-and-a-half-decade bull market!

Because of the length of this trend, many Americans have never experienced what happens to their bonds when interest rates are trending up over several years or even decades.

So, what will likely happen if interest rates do start moving back up over the next several years?

Back to our hypothetical scenario, but fast-forward a few years into the future. Your Treasury bonds are still paying you 2.54% in interest, but now we will assume interest rates have moved higher, perhaps even climbing to 4.5% (which would still be historically low).

Rising interest rates mean that the value of issued bonds will fall. How much they fall depends on several factors, including duration, or how many years remain before the bond matures.

In our scenario, interest rates have risen 77% since you bought your bonds (4.5 is 77% more than 2.54). This means that your bonds are not only underperforming compared to current rates, but if you sell them, they are now worth *significantly* less than when you bought them. (Sounds like market risk!)

So, do you sell your bonds at a discount to buy newly issued bonds paying higher interest?

Let us assume the discount is too steep for you to stomach, so you choose to hold on to your underperforming bonds with the hopes that interest rates reverse soon and start to head back down. Might happen. Or, interest rates might continue to trend higher.

Do you see the predicament you would be in?

We don't have a crystal ball, and never pretend to know what the future holds. Interest rates could stay at historic lows for many years. Then again, interest rates have cycled up and down for the past 100 years. In 2013, rates hit a *222-year* low![7]

It is worth considering the potential for serious interest rate risk losses during the foreseeable future, especially if you are in favor of fixed interest rate investments such as bonds and bond funds.

Chasing Yield and Default Risk

Default risk, as defined earlier, is when a bond issuer (borrower) is not able to return your principal at the end of the loan term, usually due to insolvency and/or bankruptcy. This risk is extremely remote when it comes to U.S. Treasury bonds but is certainly a possibility with popular, high-yield bonds (also known as junk bonds).

If you have a poor credit rating, you have to pay higher interest rates to borrow money compared to someone with an excellent credit rating. This is because on paper you are more likely to default and not make your interest payments and/or repay the principal.

This is true for companies, cities and countries with poor credit ratings, as well. If they want to borrow money (issue bonds), they must pay higher interest rates (yield) to entice lenders.

Today, because of the historically low interest rate environment, many investors are willing to accept this higher default risk for more yield, or interest. They buy debt from entities that have a higher risk of not making their payments or returning the original investment.

This risk is easy to understand. If the entity who issues the bonds becomes insolvent and is unable to pay its debts, it may file for bankruptcy. This puts the bondholders' invested principal at risk. Bondholders may be first in line to receive a settlement from bankruptcy court, but there are no guarantees they will get back all (or even most) of their principal.

What is the solution? How do you reduce your exposure to one set of risks without creating new, unmitigated risks? In other words, how do you balance these risks in a manner that works best for you, personally? That is precisely what we will cover next — finding balance.

Finding Balance with Risk vs. Reward

Have you ever come across the perfect investment? You know, the one that has:

- unlimited growth potential
- zero risk to your principal
- gives you 100% access to your money at all times
- generates a steady, dependable passive-income stream that you cannot outlive

Yeah, me neither. That is because the perfect investment does not exist. "Unlimited growth potential" and "zero risk to your principal" should have tipped you off. No such thing!

As in other areas of life, more financial reward usually comes with higher risk. It is a bit like a seesaw, with growth potential on one side and safety on the other. When growth potential is higher, safety is lower and vice versa.

As a child, did you and a friend ever try to balance a seesaw so the plank was level and both of you were off the ground at the same time? This is a great analogy for finding balance with financial risk and reward.

Growth   **Safety**

What is the appropriate mix of growth potential and safety for your accounts? The simplest way to approach this very important question is to evaluate two factors, one emotional and the other logical. These factors are your personal risk tolerance and your time horizon. Having discussed risk tolerance, let us now review "time horizon."

Time Horizon

Time horizon is fairly straightforward. You simply ask yourself, "How much time do I have before I will need or want to withdraw funds from this account?" Your answer to this is your time horizon.

For example, if you are 35 years away from retiring and will only be adding money to your retirement savings until then, you have a long time horizon with that account.

Theoretically, this means your investments can absorb higher volatility (big price swings) and market risk (lower safety) in exchange for higher growth potential.

This is because, over enough time — 15 years or more — market volatility and cycles have historically tended to smooth out and the total return of your investments can reflect the long-term market average. Not always, but usually.

Let us say, however, that you are two years away from retirement. When that happy moment arrives, you will start drawing income from one of your nest egg accounts. Your time horizon for this account is two years. Preservation of principal and liquidity (easy access to your money) logically becomes the priority, with high growth potential being the tradeoff.

This is because your investments in this account may not have enough time to recover from losses brought on by large price swings (volatility) or even a significant market downturn, should they occur in the next two years. You might get lucky and the market you are invested in continues to grow over the next two years, but that is a gamble.

[Please note that taking regular income draws from an account that is exposed to market risk and volatility exposes you to negative compounding, which is part of the sequence of returns risk. This little-known but serious risk is unique to the distribution phase of your financial life.]

The key is to determine the time horizon for each of your various retirement accounts and match them with the appropriate investments and financial tools. From a purely logical perspective, time horizon is probably the most important factor in the risk/reward tradeoff.

Summary

Hopefully, you now have a deeper understanding of risk and why proper risk mitigation and carefully balancing risk with reward are integral to successful retirement planning. Before you move on to the other important concepts in the book, though, let us revisit your three most precious assets, so you can assess your true risk tolerance.

As we discussed, your nest egg is not just a bunch of financial numbers on a statement. Your retirement assets have the power to generate passive-income streams for you. What do those passive-income streams actually represent? That is right. TIME, HEALTH and ENERGY.

Your nest egg is a bank that stores your time, your health and your life energy. No matter who you are and what else you may value, these three are your most precious assets. Without them, nothing you enjoy being, doing and having is really possible.

Once you fully grasp this, you can evaluate your true risk tolerance. With this new perspective, how much potential loss are you willing to accept with your nest egg?

It is my sincere hope that you will think long and hard on this.

And with that, let me wish you the best of success with your planning!

Chapter 11

How Conventional Wisdom May Be Failing You in Retirement

By Greg Zott

A case can be made that retirement investing is more important today than at any time in history. Why? Today's retiree is projected to live longer than any previous generation in the history of the world. Better medical care, improved nutrition and reduced manual labor are some of the many reasons for this increase in longevity. The men and women of the 21st century could live years, even as much as a decade more than their predecessors.

This is one of the wonderful results of the modern world and should bring us great joy and satisfaction. After all, increased longevity means more years to enjoy life, more opportunities to do the things we always wanted to do and see the things we always wanted to see. It also means spending more time with family, grandchildren and friends that are all so precious to us. This is the exciting new world that exists for today's retiree.

However, the joy of living longer may be tempered when you contemplate what that might mean for your retirement savings. Living longer means your money needs to last longer than ever before. Unfortunately, the majority of Americans are under-prepared when it comes to saving for their golden years.

An April 2015 survey by the Employee Benefit Research Institute demonstrates this in stark terms. It indicates 57% of retired and working Americans have less than $25,000 accumulated for their retirement years.[1] The lack of savings for retired or soon-to-be-retired individuals becomes an even bigger problem when we look at the reductions in company retirement plans. Pension plans that were available just 25 years ago are vanishing or decreasing in value throughout the workplace. In the very near future, it will be an exception, not the rule, to find a retiree with a pension that guarantees a payout for life.

Adding to these problems is lackluster stock market performance since the turn of the century. The 1980 and 1990s markets are a far cry to the nearly flat total return of stocks since January 2000. For example, in April 2015, the market celebrated an all-time record high for the Nasdaq index. What was lost in the celebration was that the last time this was achieved was March 2000. That is effectively a zero-percent return over the past 15 years. That kind of performance leads to worry for many investors, especially retirement investors.

With a lack of adequate savings, disappearing pensions and stocks treading water, is it any wonder that the exciting world of retirement is viewed with trepidation? A firm majority of Americans, 59%, are worried about not having enough money for retirement, surpassing eight other financial matters.[2] Another survey said Americans fear outliving their money more than they fear death.[3] Ironically, the great strides in longevity that have extended our golden years can also tarnish the retirement that many people worked so hard to achieve.

It seems natural that in trying times like these, we should consider using methods that seem to have a historical track record of success. These typical strategies or what the financial industry calls *conventional wisdom* would seem to be the wisest and surest course to achieve our goals. However, is that the best strategy for a retirement investor?

The reality is that conventional wisdom may fail and even work *against* you in retirement. It needs to be exposed for the traps it presents to retirees. Its benefits for retirement investors are questionable and its results can be disastrous. Most importantly, some conventional wisdom ideas must be abandoned altogether.

Advisors rarely, if ever, discuss these pitfalls associated with conventional wisdom in retirement. Why? The answer is because conventional wisdom is always good for the investment industry. Regardless of the current economic or market cycle, conventional wisdom is supposed to have the answers for us. At least that's what the financial industry tells an increasingly wary investing public.

The financial industry likes the status quo just the way it is. That is why conventional wisdom is passed on with such fervor to the general public. It is certainly easier to quote a platitude of conventional wisdom than engage in rigorous evaluation of old concepts that might require thinking outside the box.

Conventional wisdom is not always bad for the long-term investor. However, for the retired investor, it typically has no benefit in an overall retirement plan. In other words, a one-size-fits-all retirement plan that is built strictly on typical conventional wisdom, does not work for most retirees. Retirees must recognize why the underlying reasons behind conventional wisdom do not work in retirement. This is particularly important at the beginning of your retirement. The retiree who wants a successful retirement plan must be aware that conventional wisdom can hinder their retirement objectives.

Conventional Wisdom Myth #1: Buy and Hold Is the Strategy That Best Serves Stock Investors

One of the pillars of conventional wisdom is the belief that buy-and-hold investing is the only way to make money in the stock market. This approach is over 50 years old and is one of those dogmatic beliefs never to be questioned. Investors believe that it's efficient in terms of commissions and fees, and that stocks are purchased and only sold when an investor needs money, which would then reduce brokerage commissions. They also believe it's impossible to time the market, and since stocks are fairly priced, attempting to buy low and sell high is a waste of time. Buying a stock and holding on to it for the long haul is more effective.[4]

Of course, it is illegal to guarantee returns from any investment. However, the mantra that buy and hold as the only way to make money in the market is repeated so often that the disclaimer that "past performance does not guarantee future results" is basically ignored.

The S&P 500 Index rose 1,200 percent from 1980 to the end of 1999 (chart 1). Who wouldn't want to buy and hold in that market! For 20 years we had basically one trend and that trend was up, up, up! For someone working and saving toward retirement during this time, it was the era of buy and hold.

Chart 1

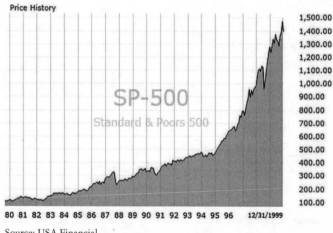

Price History

Source: USA Financial

Conventional wisdom would have us believe that the results of the last two decades of the 20th century are what to expect when you are a patient buy-and-hold investor. Of course, when you can throw a dart at a dart board and hit a winning stock, as in the 1980s and '90s, buy and hold is an excellent strategy. We need to be careful, however, to not confuse a bull market with brains.

Many of the advisors working with retirees today still view the stock market through the prism of the 1980s and '90s, the greatest bull market in history. It was indeed the greatest in history, but that is now history! With the retirees we work with today, we like to refer to that time as your father's stock market. Just as other areas of life have changed in your father's life compared to yours, the stock market of today bears no resemblance to your father's stock market (chart 2).

Chart 2

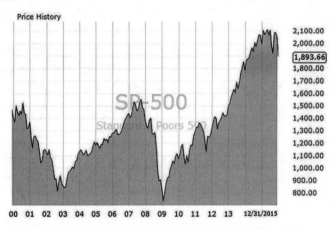

Source: USA Financial

Since the turn of the century, the buy-and-hold strategy has not held up for investors. If you had the misfortune of retiring at the peak of the market in March 2000, you would have lost half your retirement savings in less than three years. Retiring in November 2007, you would have lost half in less than 15 months. The buy-and-hold strategy would have been a gut-wrenching roller coaster ride with little benefit to your retirement savings.

During the financial crisis of 2008, our seminar attendees came to our office for meetings with sealed envelopes that held their brokerage statements. When we asked why they had not looked to see what was going on with their investments, their answers were astounding. Some stated, "My broker/advisor told me not to look because I would get upset." Others said, "My broker/advisor told me not to worry about my losses because the stock market always comes back." Does this sound familiar?

This is the mindset of the financial industry regarding the buy-and-hold philosophy. In a rising market, as in 1980-1999, any strategy is a good strategy. But in a down market, buy-and-hold offers no value. Buy and hold has no defense mechanism to help you when the market is down. Holding your investment guarantees a loss.

Another important point that the financial industry does not stress regarding the buy-and-hold strategy is the importance of time. In order for buy and hold to be successful, it may require lots of time, sometimes decades, to achieve positive results. Retirees do not have the long-term investment time frame needed to make buy and hold a viable strategy. They need to use their money now, not many years from now.

John Mauldin, a commentator and author on the markets, analyzed 88 different 20-year periods since WWII and evaluated the performance of the S&P 500 Index for these 88 time periods.[5]

He found that 50% produced annual returns of less than 4%, while less than 10% generated gains of more than 10%. Since retirees often make distributions from their portfolios during retirement, they reduce total returns even further. Mauldin's numbers indicate that historically, a buy-and-hold strategy for a large percentage of 20-year time periods achieved low, if not negative, total returns for a retirement investor.

The buy-and-hold advice that says "don't worry, your money will come back because the stock market always comes back," only has validity because the stock market has bounced back from every down cycle. That is little comfort, however, for a person who retires during a down cycle. By the time the market comes back, that retiree's savings can be wiped out or severely depleted, creating repercussions that continue throughout their lifetime.

Buy and hold never considers the ramifications of losses to your specific retirement time frame because it cannot react to a specific time frame. Buy and hold for retirement investors is like a watch stuck at 12:00. Eventually it will be right, but if you want the watch to tell you what time it is now, you better buy a new watch! Retirement is the period in your life when knowing the correct time, from a financial perspective, is most important.

Conventional Wisdom Myth #2: Asset Allocation and Rebalancing Can Increase Performance in Good Markets and Protect You in a Down Market

Another pillar of conventional wisdom is asset allocation and rebalancing. Both of these concepts are built on the belief that no one can accurately predict the market. Based on that premise, these concepts are used as a "cover all your bases" approach for investing.

Let's look at asset allocation first. Since conventional wisdom tells us that no one can predict what investment classes to be invested in at any given moment, an astute investor should be spread over many classes at all times. Thus, asset allocation spreads your dollars among various asset classes (for example, large-, mid- and small-cap stocks and bonds — domestic and international — commodities, real estate, cash) in order to balance the random nature of the market.

This theory is widely accepted in the financial industry. Armed with this strategy, an advisor designs a diversified portfolio of stocks and bonds for every investor. A portfolio using this approach is generally considered acceptable financial advice for whatever situation arises.

The second component of this myth is rebalancing. Rebalancing is a process that re-apportions your portfolio to your original asset allocation at a designated time. The typical rebalancing approach is on a specific date or dates every year, either on an annual or quarterly basis.

For example, an investor divides his $1 million into two investments (Groups A and B) worth $500,000 each. Three months later, Group

A is worth $550,000 and Group B is worth $450,000. Group A is now 55% of the portfolio and Group B is 45%. Rebalancing tells us to sell the profits from Group A and reinvest them in Group B to bring the portfolio back to its original allocation — 50% for both groups.

Did you catch that? Rebalancing states that you should "Sell better performing investments to buy lesser performing investments." The problem with this approach is that asset classes perform better than others over months and years at a time. Rarely, if ever, do they magically change on an annual or quarterly time frame. A portfolio designed to implement asset allocation and rebalancing automatically works *against* performance.

Why would we implement tools to automatically buy and sell investment classes on a prearranged schedule with no regard to the fundamentals of the investments or their value? Does this sound rational to you? Selling them arbitrarily based on this theory looks like portfolio management, but in reality it is just another way to keep money invested instead of taking profits or discarding losers based on thorough analysis.

For example, during 1995–1998, large-cap stocks outperformed small-cap stocks by a two-to-one margin and bonds by three-to-one. In 2004–2007, foreign stocks outperformed bonds by four-to-one and large stocks by nearly three-to-one. These were extended periods when one class clearly outperformed others. Why would we want to bail on these winners and reinvest in classes that were performing worse or even losing money?

The claim that asset allocation and rebalancing can reduce risk in down markets is also dubious at best. The bear market of 2000–2002 saw all asset classes, except small value stocks and bonds, take losses for not one but all three years. Similar losses in numerous investment classes occurred during bear markets over the last 50 years. It seems clear that in bear markets, unless you are out of the market altogether, or you are invested in the right asset classes, asset allocation and rebalancing do not prevent significant losses.

Just as buy and hold offers no value in a down market, asset allocation and rebalancing have no strategic advantage to a portfolio if it is applied without a specific analysis of the investments being bought and sold. This myth is used as a planning tool for all long-term investors, including retirees. However, history shows us that if applied randomly without analysis, asset allocation and rebalancing can reduce total return and increase losses in down markets. Such a scenario is worse for retirees, since portfolios are further reduced because of income withdrawals.

For the retirement investor, protecting principal is of paramount importance. Bear markets can damage or destroy your wealth. In retirement, time is no longer an ally, so losses can be more destructive and literally change your retirement plans. One of the keys to retirement investing is knowing what to buy, when to buy and most importantly, when to sell.

Harvesting profits in retirement is essential to protecting your wealth. Earning the same profits over and over again is treading water and eliminates any chance for portfolio growth. Asset allocation and rebalancing, contrary to conventional wisdom, may *prevent* a retiree from achieving the results needed to make your money outlast you in retirement.

Conventional Wisdom Myth #3: The "4% Rule" Is the Most Effective Way to Distribute Income at Retirement

In October 1994, financial advisor William Bengen published an article "Determining Withdrawal Rates Using Historical Data."[6] Bengen's theory became the guiding standard regarding post-retirement distributions in the financial industry. The 4% rule, as the theory became known, has been the conventional wisdom for retiree distributions for the past two decades.

The theory states that 4% can be safely withdrawn annually from your retirement portfolio, with an adjustment for inflation over a 30-year time span. Once again, the buy-and-hold strategy is prominent to this thesis. Bengen postulated that a 50–50 mix of stocks and bonds, held over this period, would generate enough gains to cover the 4% withdrawal rate with little loss of principal.

It is interesting to note that Bengen's theory became popular in the latter stages of the greatest bull market in history. After 1994, the year Bengen proposed his theory, the S&P 500 gained 144% and bonds rose over 40% through the end of the 20th century. Retirement investors who used the 4% rule for their distributions in the final years of the 1990s were successful and satisfied with the results. It also made post-retirement distribution planning much easier for the financial industry.

There was no need to make analytical or strategic changes to a portfolio. To quote Bengen, "The analysis supports the view that a 4% withdrawal rate with the suggested investment mix is a *safe distribution plan* for retirement." Much like buy and hold, this concept allows the advisor to "set it and forget it" when it comes to distribution planning. The 4% rule masquerades as a well-thought-out distribution plan for retirees.

The truth is the stock and bond returns after 1994 made the 4% rule a safe distribution plan, not the theory itself. When total returns are more than nine times the rate of withdrawal, there is little risk to the principal. During the latter part of the 1990s, many retirees were encouraged to withdraw sums well above 4%. Since markets performed so well during this time, the excess withdrawals had no effect on principal. Conventional wisdom assured retirees that a buy-and-hold approach, coupled with the 4% rule, was the formula for a successful retirement plan.

The market crashes of 2000–2002 and 2008 brought the success of this strategy under intense scrutiny. In 2013, the 4% rule was examined by researchers Dr. Michael Finke, Dr. Wade Pfau and Morningstar's David Blanchett. They found that when Bengen's theory was subject to the economic and market conditions of the 21st century, the acclaimed 4% rule had an astounding failure rate of 57%! Examples from the study saw more than half of the retirees using the 4% rule for post-retirement distributions had run out of money in the first 15 years of retirement! Despite these startling statistics, the financial industry as a whole still uses this myth for today's retirees.

Before a retiree can determine what dollar or percentage amount can be distributed from his plan, a number of questions need to be asked. For example, is the retiree comfortable with the 50/50 stock and bond investment mix? Do market conditions warrant a higher percentage in stocks? Are market conditions better for a higher percentage in bonds? Are withdrawals constant, or will they be higher or lower in the early years of retirement? How will Social Security payments factor into the overall distribution? Does the distribution plan account for future inflation?

In retrospect, the 4% rule offers no strategic value. It seems foolish to establish a specific withdrawal percentage without first answering these questions and examining the economic and market conditions a retiree must navigate through.

If history repeats itself, bear markets will be experienced by retirees. Since 1929, the U.S. stock market has experienced 25 bear markets, an average of one every 3.4 years.[7] A 65-year-old retiree who lives until age 90 could experience a handful of bear markets during his post-retirement years. If that holds true for the next generation of retirees, the 4% rule has a much better chance of failing than securing income that will outlast a lifetime.

Conventional Wisdom Myth #4: Educated and Well-Informed Investors Make Prudent Decisions About Investing

Exposing why conventional wisdom can be detrimental, if not dangerous, to a retiree is extremely important. Over 90% of our clients are in retirement or will be in just a few years. Many of my relatives and friends are reaching these critical years without the knowledge of how these concepts may destroy their golden years. The more people that understand why buy and hold, asset allocation, rebalancing and the 4% rule can be devastating to their retirement plans, the better equipped they will be to deal with the unique longevity issues that affect today's retirees.

Conventional wisdom tells us that an educated, well-informed investor makes intelligent choices and is prudent in his investment thinking. As a financial advisor, we strive to make all our clients knowledgeable investors. Knowledge is power and a client who understands their investment plan is more likely to implement all its steps and stay on course.

However, putting that knowledge to practical use in your portfolio is not as easy as it sounds. Why? Because human beings are very emotional creatures. Go figure! Regardless of how knowledgeable an investor is, emotional behavior is still the overriding factor in investment decision-making. How do we know this?

For two decades, a Boston research firm named Dalbar has released an annual report known as the "Quantitative Analysis of Investment Behavior." This fascinating study is filled with information about why investors do what they do. The answers continue to turn conventional wisdom on its head. The knowledgeable, well-informed investor is not very rational. "Passive management" — another name for the buy and hold — plays havoc with our emotions. And these emotions, in turn, negatively affect investor results.

The report covers 30 calendar years, 1985 through 2014. This includes the one-day market crash of 1987, the 1990s bull market and the bear markets of the 21st century, as well as their subsequent recoveries. The data computes an "average" investor return, based on purchases and liquidations by regular investors. These average returns are compared with results of mutual funds themselves and of common indexes for stock and bond funds.[8] In those 30 calendar years, Standard & Poor's 500 Index compounded at 11%. In that same period, the average mutual fund investor achieved a return of only 3.7%. That's not a misprint. Individual investors actually earned barely more than a third of what they could have earned.[9] The numbers remain poor, no matter the time frame. During the past 20 calendar years, the index was up 9%, while the average investor earned only 5%. In the past 10 years, the S&P 500 was up 7.4%, and the average investor's return was 5.9%.[10] In fact, in every year of Dalbar's research, investors earn less than the market or their corresponding mutual fund performance, sometimes much less.

Every Dalbar report indicates that emotionally based investor responses reduce total return performance for a portfolio. Furthermore, Dalbar's main conclusion is that no matter whether we are in a bull or bear market, investor results are more dependent on emotional behavior than on any other factor. This can be illustrated in "The Cycle of Investor Emotions."

Chart 3

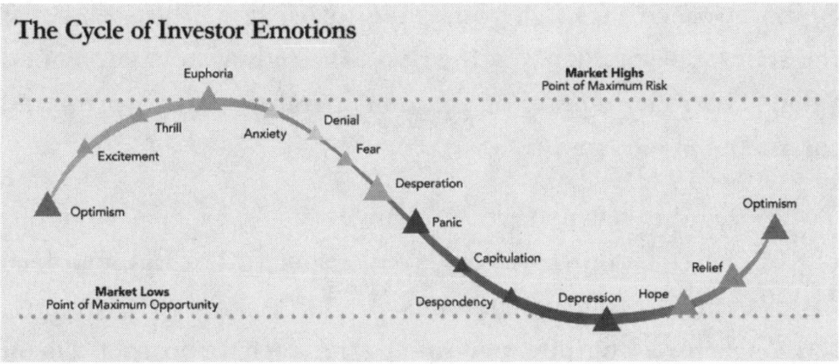

The Cycle of Investor Emotions

Source: USA Financial

No amount of education or knowledge trumps the emotional responses on this roller coaster ride that all human beings experience whenever they began investing. As the value of an investor's portfolio peaks, his emotions reach a state of *euphoria*. At that point in time, he has never felt better about his portfolio. Statistics tell us that this is the time when investors are adding more money to their portfolios than any other. Notice that at the time of euphoria, however, investors are at what is known as the point of maximum financial risk. A well-informed, prudent decision would be to take profits; our emotions tell us to go for broke.

At the bottom of the emotional cycle is the state of mind between despondency and depression. At this point in time, you have never felt worse about your portfolio. It is not coincidental that this is the time when money is least likely to be invested. This emotional trough, however, coincides with the point of maximum financial opportunity. A prudent investor would indeed "buy low." Unfortunately, due to our emotions, it takes a steely resolve to invest when everything is plunging into the abyss. The average investor rarely, if ever, has such resolve.

The cycle of investor emotions is misunderstood by the financial industry. Instead of using the cycle to buy (despondency) and sell (euphoria), they use the cycle to convince investors to hold their investments indefinitely. They never see that the state of euphoria on chart 3 is a good time to harvest profits and that the state of despondency is the best time to buy stocks at a good value. The roller coaster of emotions paralyzes the investor and the financial industry.

Therefore, the key to successful investing is to take emotions out of the equation. Investors need a specific, logical approach to investing, devoid of emotions. If this is important for pre-retirement investing, how much more critical is it for post-retirement investing? Retirement investors, as mentioned previously, have little time to make up for emotional mistakes.

We have shown that conventional wisdom has limits to its application for the retirement investor. In fact, it can be more than a limitation. In some instances, it can outright destroy your plans for a safe and prosperous retirement. Perhaps the best choice for a retirement investor is not to embrace conventional wisdom but to first have a plan. Once the plan is established, we can then implement some often ignored traditional strategies that have existed for many years. These strategies offer value to the retiree in all market and economic conditions.

The Asset Cycle Portfolio System®: A Strategic Distribution Plan

Many advisors do not recognize the significance between pre- and post-retirement investing. We have heard it said that everything changes in retirement. If so, why would an investor not consider a change in his investment strategy?

In pre-retirement, a long-term time frame is the working model and it is focused entirely on growth. However, in post-retirement the focus shifts to both growing and preserving our assets. This joint focus is critical for post-retirement planning. The strategic advantage of having many years to recoup investment losses is gone. So the planning must change to your changing situation.

To grow and preserve assets, an analysis of specific investments, as well as an assessment of the existing market cycle, is crucial before constructing a plan. In retirement, assets are more than just accumulated dollars. They are the retiree's income source for the rest of his or her life.

A strategy we have found that helps recognize the significance of this change is to treat your retirement assets like a business. A business needs to be profitable short term and have a vision for long-term growth. In the same way, a retirement plan must use assets for day-to-day operations (immediate income) and others for long-term growth (investments). The overriding goal of this business is to provide the employer (you) a paycheck for life. How is this done? Let's look at the illustration known as the "bucket approach."

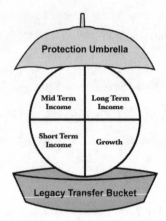

Source: USA Financial

Your assets, like employees of a business, are assigned specific jobs that fulfill a role within your retirement plan. For example, the short-term income employee is like a company's production worker; he generates income on a day-to-day basis. The mid-term and long-term income employees are like a company's mid and upper management. Their goal is to ensure growth in the company for the next five to 10 years. The growth account employee is the CEO. His job is to increase the overall business value so that day-to-day activities (income) can continue well into the future.

The protection umbrella is like insurance for a company. In a retirement plan, this is equivalent to providing a need to cover long-term care expenses, if they arise during the life of the retiree. Lastly, the legacy bucket is the business transfer to the company heirs. This is applicable to making sure that retirement assets or life insurance proceeds pass on to loved ones in the most efficient tax manner possible.

The bucket approach strategy was first developed by financial planner Harold Evensky in the 1980s. Since then, variations have been added, but the basics remain intact. The buckets will usually cover five-year periods, with the last bucket replacing assets after 15 years of growth. The specific strategy or investment vehicle will be determined by the job description in each bucket.

This approach has two important aspects. First, it is a distribution plan, not just an arbitrary withdrawal of income to live on. Secondly, it offers peace of mind to retirees. There is no need to worry if the stock market goes up or down in a given week, month or year. Because this plan designates and protects assets for short- and mid-term income, a retiree can lay his head on his pillow at night and not worry if the market goes up or down. The plan ensures that his income needs for the first five years will not be disturbed.

For our clients, the benefit of this system was dramatic during the 2008 financial crisis. They were spared the catastrophic losses that retirees who used the conventional wisdom strategies experienced. The devastating reality for many retirees was that their traditional post-retirement plans had no defense mechanism at the time of the crisis. For some, it was a time when they realized their future lifestyle had changed forever.

The financial industry continues to use the conventional wisdom idea that buy and hold, coupled with the 4% distribution plan, is the wise and prudent approach. The misery of 2008 is just a bad memory that has little emotional impact today. However, continuing with the same retirement strategy that failed in 2008 reminds me of the following definition of insanity:

"Doing the same things over and over and expecting different results."

The conventional wisdom concepts of buy and hold for all markets and the 4% rule for post-retirement distribution planning are part of the financial industry's insanity. We want to warn today's retirees that these approaches will not work when the next 2008 occurs.

Strategies Beyond Buy and Hold: Value Investing

Retirees in 2015 face the dilemma of whether or not their money will outlast them. As previously mentioned, the only solution much of the financial industry offers is the conventional wisdom of buy-and-hold investing. Retirees are betting their retirement — and the remainder of their financial life — on this pillar of conventional wisdom.

The industry spends hundreds of millions of dollars annually acquiring information designed to improve investment decisions. However, in the end, the knowledge gained from this research is harder to use than implementing the conventional wisdom approach of buy and hold. In addition, buy and hold gives the financial industry a second chance at mistakes because it is the accepted approach for investing.

What is interesting is that many of the pioneers of the investment world *did not* employ the conventional wisdom of buy and hold throughout their careers. Contrary to conventional wisdom, they used analytical skills and various historical criteria to achieve extraordinary success in stock investing. They left a legacy of ideas for investing that are used far too infrequently as alternatives to buy and hold.

Benjamin Graham, the "father of value investing," is considered the greatest mind in the history of investing. His book, *The Intelligent Investor*, is also considered the most important book ever written on the subject. Warren Buffett attributes many of his investment skills to the knowledge gleaned from Graham.

Graham bought stocks based on a fundamental analysis of their value and sold them when their market price reached close to what he considered their business value. Long-term time frames were irrelevant; when analysis and price coincided, he took profits. One of his most profound investment quotes is crucial for the retirement investor. "Confronted with a challenge to distill the secret of sound investment into three words, we venture the motto, Margin of Safety."

John Templeton was a legendary investor who founded the Franklin Templeton Investment Group. His investment approach was also value based. One of his core principles was that investors must know when to sell. He always took profits when valuations were high based on his analysis. He often remarked that investors gave up profits time and again because they had no clear definition of real value for their investments.

Seth Klarman is considered by some as the Warren Buffett of the baby boomer generation. Klarman's book, *Margin of Safety: Risk-Averse Value Investing Strategies for the Thoughtful Investor*, explains his value approach to investing. For retirement investors, one quote from the book stands out. "Interestingly, we have beaten the market quite handsomely … but beating the market has never been our objective. Rather, we have consistently tried **not to lose money** (emphasis is mine) by assessing the value of the stocks we bought and knowing when to sell them. In doing so, we have not only protected on the downside but also outperformed on the upside."

It's clear from these financial gurus that *assessing value* on particular stocks has produced success. It's also interesting that all of the above had specific criteria for both *buying and selling* a stock. The idea that stocks would be held long term without regard to their value is the opposite of what they practiced.

These pioneers had strategies based on specific criteria and learned to evaluate the value of their investments and made changes accordingly. If the value of their holdings reached the levels they determined were their optimum value, the stocks were sold. All three men had a plan that indicated when it is a good time to buy, a good time to hold and a good time to sell.

Strategies Beyond Buy and Hold: Relative Strength

Relative strength analysis (RSA) is another alternative strategy to buy and hold. The logic behind RSA is that individual stocks stay strong for weeks or months at a time. Therefore, stocks are assigned benchmarks that determine when they will be bought and sold. In other words, the highest ranked stocks in a particular index should be bought and held until they lose momentum below a pre-determined relative strength ranking. Because this is a frequent occurrence, stocks are never held for long periods of time, contrary to a buy-and-hold strategy.

In his book, *Buy—Don't Hold*, Leslie Masonson put together what he called a "dashboard" of indicators that documented the superior total returns achieved with relative strength versus buy and hold over many decades. Author James O'Shaughnessy in *What Works on Wall Street*, studied relative strength analysis and concluded the strategy outperformed buy and hold for the last 45 years. Just like value investing, relative strength is a strategy that indicates when it is a good time to buy, a good time to hold and a good time to sell.

When we discussed the conventional wisdom concepts of asset allocation and rebalancing, we showed that classes and sectors of stocks remain strong for long periods of time. This is why annual or quarterly resetting can actually *reduce* total returns in a portfolio. The same reasoning applies to relative strength with individual stocks. Some stocks will outperform the overall class or sector for long periods of time. Relative strength is an approach an investor can use to get the best returns for as long as possible, while at the same time knowing a specific time when that stock should be sold.

Strategies Beyond Buy and Hold: Market Trending

Lastly, we want to discuss the impact of historical stock cycles on a portfolio. In his book *Stock Cycles*, Michael Alexander demonstrates that there are certain long-term cycles that are not random. These secular bull and bear market cycles can last for decades and have appeared one after another for over 200 years since the year 1800. Understanding how these cycles work is crucial for the retiree when developing a successful investment plan.

There are a number of significant points to make regarding these secular cycles. According to Alexander, you need to first understand that a secular cycle is never a short-term trend. In fact, he found no statistical evidence that a secular cycle could predict whether the market would be up or down in a 12-month period. The term "secular" is specifically used since this means an age or an era, thus distinguishing it from a regular bull or bear market, which are much shorter periods. He also points out that the secular cycles can vary in length and are not precisely predictable.

However, his research did show that in every secular cycle over two centuries, the market trend of the cycle was constant. If the cycle was a secular bull, the trend was up; if a secular bear, the trend was down. Although there were months and even years when the market went in the opposite direction, the cycle always reverted to its bull or bear trend before its completion.

This historical fact is why retirees must consider the overall direction of the current market cycle in retirement investing.

Charts 4 and 5 demonstrate what secular cycles look like. You can clearly see the difference in trends between 1980–2000 versus 2000–2015.

Chart 4

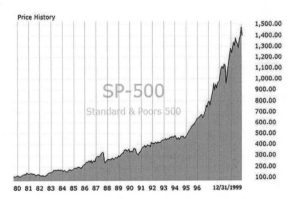

Chart 5

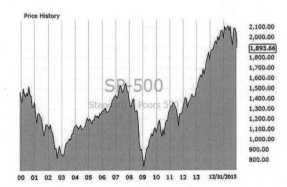

Source: USA Financial

In this sense, this strategy is analogous to farming. A successful farmer knows that spring is the planting season and that fall is time for the harvest. For the investor, there is a time to plant (investing and holding) and a time to harvest (profit-taking). Unfortunately, many advisors who work with retirement investors do not know what season it is. Further, the bias of buy and hold makes the importance of defining the season irrelevant. If you are constantly investing and holding, why bother knowing when or if it is a good time to take profits?

Consider the ramifications of using the buy-and-hold strategy in a secular bear market cycle. Historically, such a cycle would seem to indicate an overall downward trend in the market. If you are a retirement investor, can you afford to invest in a plan that has no system for evaluating if the trend is no longer in your favor? Market trending is the defense mechanism that every retiree needs in his plan. I believe examining where the trend is headed has real value for clients.

It is important to note the difference between "market timing" and "market trending." Market timing is an effort to time the highs and lows of the market. It is always playing catch-up, chasing the next good trade or the next uptick. This strategy has proven unsuccessful over multiple time frames and up and down markets. In fact, the abysmal performance of market timers by investors — and some money managers — is one of the reasons buy and hold is so vociferously touted by the financial industry.

Market trending on the other hand, never attempts to predict or react to the market on a short-term basis. Instead, it examines long-term trends to potentially increase your odds for long-term success. Just as an extended weather forecast can't guarantee a beautiful day, it can decrease your chance of a stormy one.

Final Thoughts

We began the chapter by acknowledging that the life of a 21st century retiree will be longer than any in the history of the world. That is a wonderful and sobering thought. The wonder will be enhanced exponentially if those years are supported by a retirement plan that navigates successfully through good times and bad.

As the stock market is now through its seventh year of positive gains, complacency may lull retirees into believing that conventional wisdom will serve them well in the years to come. Instead, retirees must recognize the inherent pitfalls of conventional wisdom regarding retirement planning. Before the pillars of conventional wisdom fail you in retirement, we urge you to re-examine your retirement plan so that you can be confident that your money will outlast you.

Chapter 12

Addressing the Long-Term Health Care Threat With Lazy Assets

By Barry Waronker, JD

Who Really Pays for Long-Term Care?

Even if you don't want to think about long-term care for yourself, think about what the experience can do to your family. Although the conversation about long-term care tends to focus on the potential financial disaster, experience has shown that the price is more than dollars and cents. We've heard time and again that if you are a family caregiver, you are at a greater health risk than the loved one you are caring for. The fact is, when you are devoting your time and energy to the needs of another, there is a tendency to neglect your own needs. Caregivers often don't see the difficulty of the situation. They know they're stressed, but they often don't recognize the direct effect that stress can have on their own health.

Some facts:

- 45% of caregivers reported chronic conditions versus 24% for non-caregivers.[1]
- Caregivers average four doctor visits per year versus seven for non-caregivers.[2]
- Levels of IL-6, a substance that hinders immune system function, was four times higher among elderly caregivers vs. non-caregivers.[3]
- Family caregivers who had a high level of responsibility had a 51% incidence of sleeplessness.[4]

- Elderly caregiving spouses (aged 66-96) who experience caregiving-related stress have a 63% higher mortality rate than non-caregivers of the same age.[5]

That's something to think about, isn't it?

I Really Don't Want to Think About It

Sure, you'd rather think about anything else than one day needing long-term care. It's a lot more fun to look through colorful travel brochures and picture all the wonderful experiences that you'd like the coming years to bring. Let's put that brochure down for a few minutes and consider what not having long-term care means — it's a risk that can wipe out a lifetime of savings and investments and can take a huge mental and physical toll on the people you care most about.

Seriously, how are you going to handle it?

I'll Just Pay for It Out of Savings

Great idea. In theory. The problem is that you are looking at an average annual nursing home cost of $80,300 for a semi-private room.[6] The majority of long-term care costs occur in your 80s, so if you're 60 years old today, you're most likely to need care at age 80 and up. Assuming 3.5% for inflation over the next 20 years, you could be looking at about $160,600 per year or $480,000 for a three-year stay.

With life expectancies in the mid-80s and a 50% chance that one member of a couple will reach their 90s, the cost could be even higher.[7] Unless you put aside that kind of liquid money, self-insurance isn't practical. Long-term care insurance has been around for over 40 years, so why don't you already own this kind of protection?

I Won't Go to a Nursing Home ... I'll Be Cared for at Home

Just about everyone would prefer care at home, and studies show that people do better in familiar surroundings. The majority of claims begin at home with costs for homemaker services and home health aides averaging $125 to $127 per day or $46,000 annually. Other services such as adult day health care run about $68 per day or $17,600 annually. If you need more care than you can get at home but not at the level provided at nursing, then assisted-living facilities can bridge the gap at $119 per day or $43,500 per year.[8]

Many policies provide a pool of money that can be used to reimburse all or some of the cost of these services. For example, a policy with a pool of $288,000 could pay up to $6,000 per month for covered services. If you used it to the max, the money would run out in four years. But if your costs are $3,000 a month, say for home care or assisted living, that policy would last eight years. Experts note that people often start with home care and then move through different levels of care to meet their needs.

If I Never Use the Insurance, I Will Have Wasted All That Money!

You are right. As you move into and through your retirement years, you're probably doing all you can to lower expenses. Does it really make sense to pay year after year to protect against something that may never happen? One very successful long-term care specialist I spoke to told me that these policies have gotten harder and harder to sell, and convincing people to take on a new obligation in retirement — and the higher premiums on new policies — are only part of the reason. There is a bigger problem.

You Will Know What You Are Buying. You Won't Know What You Are Paying.

There's a powerful reason more people are unwilling to take on the annual monthly payments for long-term care insurance: Every insurance carrier has had to go to some of their existing policyholders and inform them that, like it or not, their premium was going up. Some have raised rates more than once.

Imagine you buy a $300,000 house and finance it with a 30-year mortgage of $1,000 a month. Five years later your mortgage company says your new payment is $1,350. In effect, that is what's happened to many long-term care policyholders.

Picture yourself in 10 or 15 years. You bought a traditional long-term care policy at what you considered a reasonable price. Now you get a letter from your insurance carrier informing you that your premium is going up by 25%. At that point you have three choices: Accept the increase, reduce your coverage or drop the policy. If you are 70 or 80 years old, or older, none of those options are appealing.

A Common Sense Strategy

Consider a different way to approach the problem, one that allows you to buy the protection of long-term care benefits — and have the comfort of knowing that whether you ever need care or not, your premium dollars will not be wasted. This approach allows you to leverage a lazy asset into a new kind of protection — one that combines the best features of life insurance and long-term care into one universal life insurance contract. And by lazy, it means that the money isn't working in the best way for you that it should be.

Assuming you are healthy enough to qualify, you pay a single premium and not a penny more. Ever. Your single premium secures a death benefit **and** provides an accelerated death benefit rider to pay out long-term care benefits, if needed. Best of all, some policies allow a 100% refund of the premium should you decide you no longer want or need the protection.

Policies vary from company to company and state to state, but here is an example of how it can work. Mary is 60 years old and in good health. Knowing the potential cost of long-term care, she's kept $150,000 in a low-interest savings account "just in case." But really, how many years will that last if her expenses are running $80,000 a year? And if she needs care at age 80 with a projected cost of over $160,000 a year, what then?

Mary Moves Her Lazy Asset ... and Uses It to Protect Her Nest Egg

There are many examples of asset-based, long-term care policies and they will differ for everyone because they are based on the client's age, gender, marital status, health and if it's offered in your state. Occasionally there is other underwriting criteria that is considered before determining if a person qualifies for insurance. Here's one example: Mary moves $100,000 from her lazy money savings account and puts it into a single premium universal life policy with accelerated death benefits for long-term care. If she needs long-term care, her $100,000 is leveraged to provide meaningful help; she will have access to $262,934 in benefits to provide home care, assisted living and nursing home care. And the benefit is growing 3% a year.

If she passes away without needing long-term care, her heirs receive a guaranteed income tax-free death benefit. Best of all, if she changes her mind before accessing her benefits, this policy even allows her to receive a 100% return of her premiums. The following is an example only and not representative of a specific product.

Before		After	
Savings Account	$150,000	Savings Account	$ 50,000
Death Benefit	0	Income Tax-Free Death Benefit	$125,806
Long-Term Care	0	Long-Term Care	$262,934
		Long-Term Care at Age 80	$474,888

If you've been sitting on your lazy assets (or have cash value in a previously permanent life insurance policy) this is worth looking into. If you need care you, will have made a good choice. If you never need care, your money will go to the people you care most about.

Chapter 13

Hiring a Financial Advisor: What You Need to Know

By David Swanson

The process of selecting an advisor can seem challenging.

By following these basic rules, you will be assured you are making the best possible choice for you and your family in developing an income distribution plan customized to your lifestyle.

We will get to the set of rules in a minute.

To start off — if you are fortunate enough to have a referral to an advisor, you are miles ahead of those trolling the internet for the catch of the day. The referral should be a good place to begin your selection process. Be sure to understand the strengths and weaknesses of the advisor as your colleague has detailed them. But, of course, keep in mind these are opinions from your friends. Have an open mind and plan for a "get to know you meeting" during your first encounter.

If you are not fortunate enough to have a referral, you will be on your own to properly evaluate and interview the professional(s) you are considering. It may be wise to conduct a background check on an advisor before the first meeting.

This is where the internet can be extremely powerful in researching prospective advisors.

One place to visit is BrokerCheck.com, a site developed by the Financial Industry Regulatory Authority (FINRA). This is widely viewed as a go-to website for anyone, including the U.S. Securities and Exchange Commission (SEC) registered investment professionals. If you cannot find the advisor, look to the states' website in which the firm is located, as some companies are regulated at the state level. If information on the company does not appear in either of these locations, find out why before any further due diligence is performed.

Many non-governmental sites can also provide useful information. Try the Better Business Bureau (bbb.org), the National Ethics Association (ethics.net) or the Financial Planning Association (oneFPA.org). This list is designed to be a starting point.

If the advisor you are considering has a derogatory comment or something disclosed on their record, it doesn't *necessarily* mean you shouldn't consider hiring them. You'll simply want to do a little more investigating to make sure you understand the big picture first, and you'll certainly want to ask some questions so you can make the proper evaluation. Think of it like this — most restaurants that have been around for a while will receive negative reviews at some point (especially with the internet these days). A negative review on a restaurant doesn't necessarily mean the food is bad. With that said, selecting the right financial advisor is far more important and involved than determining where you should eat your next meal.

Another way, and in my opinion perhaps one of the best, is to attend a workshop or seminar that they conduct.

This is a no-commitment, quasi-introductory appointment. It is a great way to be introduced to the philosophy, demeanor and skill-set of the presenter. As I will point out in the rules section of this chapter, your personal feelings, I mean that strong first impression, will frame the entire relationship going forward. If you have a poor first impression, it most likely is right to keep looking.

Rules

First meeting
1. Trust your instincts
2. Independent vs. captive
3. Verify competency
4. Communications style
5. Planning philosophy
6. Action plan

Second meeting
7. Examine work product, reports and documentation
8. Discuss fees
9. Detail services provided and by whom
10. Succession plan for advisor

Third meeting

By this time, you should have a good idea if this is the correct planner for you.

First meeting

Rule #1 – Trust your instincts

You never get a second chance to make a first impression. The origin of the phrase is a bit unclear, and it's either attributed to performer Will Rogers or poet and novelist Oscar Wilde.

Truer words have never been spoken. As an advisor who conducts many public workshops each year, I am painfully aware of how the message can be lost when your presentation is off.

A projector or sound-system failure can create a bad first impression.

I have been delivering presentations for nearly two decades, and there have been some memorable bad first impressions. At this one particular event we had an audience of 125 people. Just as I started the workshop, the laptop failed. It took the next 15 minutes working feverishly to regain control of the cyborg, and during this time several couples exited the event. Now that is one instance of a bad first impression.

Often a bad first impression cannot be defined in terms of an event, but more in terms of a feeling. In almost every planning session I ask, "How do you feel?" It should be very important to the advisor that you are feeling good about the prospects for your future and in the terms of the process being discussed. If not, do not schedule another appointment.

I often find couples have very different skill-sets. Some are very analytical and some are more in touch with the perspectives of life. Women generally tend to be deeper thinkers, and after our initial discussions I ask for the couple to consider carefully the key points of the meeting and allow the deeper thinker's instincts to guide the couple to the next phase of the planning process.

Rule #2 – Independent vs. captive

The structure of the firm you choose will have a great effect on the ultimate outcome of your plan.

The company's structure is set up in two ways: independent or captive. As a retirement planning professional for over three decades, I have been on both sides of the coin (captive and independent).

I spent the first 10 years of my career as a captive advisor. During that span, I worked for two of the largest and best known Wall Street brokerage firms. All brokerage houses/banks have a menu of investment options the client may choose from. This menu or these product options are designed, in part, around profit — the profit to the firm. In many cases, as was my personal experience, a captive advisor is prohibited from offering investment options outside of the firm's menu options. As any ethical advisor would agree, the client's best interests must always be at the forefront of any investment plan.

Herein lies the conflict. If you are an ethical financial professional and work as a captive representative of a firm with a limited set of product options, how can your clients' best interests be served? The captive advisor, in many cases, is forced into a product sales role. Their focus may be more on keeping their job while pushing the product of the day. This was my personal experience. After 10 years, I woke up one day and decided I simply could not sell another "top rated" fund the firm was pitching.

I left and formed my own firm. As an independent investment advisor, I now have the luxury of planning first and investing second. The hopes and desires of the clients are not constrained by the limited choices of your typical captive brokerage firm. I firmly believe that the creation, design and implementation of the optimal retirement savings plan cannot be achieved with a limit to your investment selections.

Rule #3 – Verify competency

Understanding the credentials and experience of the advisor is a mission-critical factor in achieving your desired goals. Check out the licensures and certifications of the individual. At a minimum, they need to be federally and/or state licensed to provide the desired services. The licensure check will also allow you to view any disclosed complaints or regulatory issues that may have occurred. Scouring the internet for information about your prospective advisor may assist you in the evaluation process.

After you have completed your regulatory review of the advisor and the firm, you are ready to look at their longevity and specific disciplines in the advisory field.

How long have they been providing retirement planning services? Yes, you are looking for a resume of sorts. Much of this data can be gleaned from the firm's website or regulatory disclosure. The advisor needs to tell you in their own words what they have done and what services they provide. If you are not satisfied or your intuition light is flashing red, select another advisor.

Rule #4 – Communications style

How are you spoken to? Are you a student in a classroom or a partner in the planning process? After all, this is your life savings we are talking about, so you better get the communication right.

There are two main types of advisors, and they are those who:
- Tell you what they want you to do
- Ask what you want

In the first of these meetings, you should be asked about your goals and objectives, your hopes and dreams for the future, and in the certainty of your death, how you wish to have your assets distributed.

If an advisor attempts to offer products before your retirement planning needs have been discussed, this should be another red flag. You very well may be sitting in front of a salesperson acting as an advisor.

Rule #5 – Planning philosophy

I have always said, "If you do not have a plan, it matters little which road you choose to travel." After your goals and objectives have been discussed, a plan or road map to accomplish those priorities must be designed. This road map must be brief and simply written. While some of the investment vehicles used in the plan may be complex or sophisticated, you will want to make sure that you can understand it. This understanding will give you a greater sense of confidence in the plan itself. A good rule of thumb is that after the advisor has gathered the necessary personal and financial information and presented the written plan, you should be able to explain the plan to any trusted associate, family member, or friend with confidence. If the plan is incomplete or too convoluted, another red flag should be waving. One identifier that separates product sales representatives and retirement planning professionals is the creation of this written plan; without it, you may be at the mercy of the next best product to be offered.

Rule #6 – Action plan

Now you should be close to the conclusion of the first meeting. This meeting in general should not take more than one hour. Adults can focus on a subject for about 20 minutes before a reset is required, thus in a one-hour meeting your focus has been lost and reset three times.[1] My general observation is that after 60 minutes very little is accomplished. In addition to getting to know one another a little better, the goal of that first meeting should be to have the advisor articulate an action plan for future meetings. If a product or investment is offered during that first meeting, it's far more likely that you've encountered a salesperson, not a comprehensive advisor.

By this time, the meeting is ending and the next appointment should be scheduled. If your intent is not to meet again, a polite "Thank you very much. I want to think about it." response will usually get you out the door without too much pain. If you feel pressured to act on a recommendation, politely decline and head for the exit. Remember, we're not talking about purchasing a pair of jeans — we're talking about your financial future!

Second meeting

Rule #7 – Examine work product, reports and documentation

At this point, you should feel a bit more comfortable and in sync with the advisor. An exchange of personal and financial data should have already occurred, as the advisor must have this data to prepare for the next meeting with you.

At this meeting, the advisor should be able to present an understandable and concise written road map of the value they can bring to your situation. They should explain to you the concerns and threats that exist within your current financial situation, as well as outline some of the main opportunities that exist for you to potentially capture. Furthermore, they should explain the planning services that will help you to address those concerns and realize those opportunities. To help you better understand the services, an advisor may share with you some examples of his/her work from past clients. These examples should have client ages, assets, incomes and expense budgets similar to your situation, and should be for the next 30-40 years. It does very little to review a $5 million financial plan when you have $500,000 in retirement savings. If the presented reports are not relatively close to your envisioned retirement plan, this advisor has missed something and you'll probably want to move in another direction. Yes, this is another red flag. These reports should detail the precise income streams from all investment resources, coordinate Social Security and pension distributions, and incorporate outside income sources such as consulting/wages or rentals, and include spending needs and anticipate reasonable, extra expenses going forward.

If you like the work product, the advisor will be able to use the information you provided supplemented with additional data and create the same type of plan for you.

You may be wondering — what is this plan going to cost?

Rule #8 – Discuss fees

Two of the most common questions that clients have at this moment in the process are, "How much do you charge for your services?" and "What happens if you die (or retire)?" We will discuss fees here and address the business transition issue in Rule #10.

Fees, charges and commissions — it doesn't matter what you call them, just identify them.

Your advisor had better be able to clearly detail all investment and custodial costs and expenses associated with the planning and investment process.

If the advisor cannot satisfactorily answer all your questions about fees and cost, they might be hiding something or giving you half-truths. Trust your instincts, as it may be another red flag.

How a financial professional is paid is really dependent on the financial licenses they hold and the recommendations they are providing as a part of the plan.

A commission broker charges per transaction. This type of financial professional typically maintains a Series 6 or 7 license (see BrokerCheck. org for more details). Compensation is typically received in the form of a commission on the transaction amount.

If an advisor maintains an insurance license, they may also be compensated via commissions for insurance or fixed annuity recommendations.

The biggest concern of working with a financial professional who is compensated in this manner is the potential for a conflict of interest. They may be more incentivized to do more transactions/trades in order to generate commissions again; these transactions may or may not be in your best interests.

When an advisor has a sales manager or boss that is breathing down their neck to generate more revenue for the firm, it's very easy to see how this can present a conflict of interest between the client's needs and the pressure to make sales. Speaking from personal experience working at two large brokerage firms, there was constant pressure to sell more products, generate more commissions and earn more money. It is important that you know how your advisor is compensated on each of the transactions they are recommending for your plan.

A fee-based or fee-only advisors' compensation is based on a percentage of the assets that are directly managed. One advantage to these types of accounts is that they help an advisor stay objective, as the recommendations within the portfolio don't command a different compensation.

In addition to being compensated by commission or as a percentage of assets under management, some advisors may charge a fee for the creation and development of a financial plan. They may use an engagement agreement to establish the services that will be performed, which will correspond with their planning fee. A typical plan may require anywhere from four to six hours to complete. The fee you may pay will likely vary depending upon the services provided, complexity of the situation, experience of the advisor, and region of the country. A well-trained professional will adjust the plan as necessary through the entire process.

There isn't necessarily a right or wrong way to pay for the advice you receive, so long as you receive value.

Former president Ronald Reagan once said "Trust, but verify."[2] This is especially true when it comes to matters regarding your finances. If you find a professional you feel you can trust — that's wonderful. But you should always verify things to make sure they are doing what they said they would. This is especially true when it comes to paying for services and advice.

Rule #9 – Detail services provided and by whom

Now that you know what the planning process consists of and what it will cost for these services, we can move on. Who do you talk with to get help with your money?

To start, you must have an understanding of who will be providing your advice and service. This knowledge is essential. Some advisors will assign your account management and maintenance to a junior advisor in the office. Working with a junior advisor may not be such a bad idea, because they might be more responsive to your needs and thus provide a greater level of service than a more senior advisor with a greater number of commitments. It is ultimately your choice, so make it wisely.

Most offices have two main divisions — operations and advisory. You'll want to know who handles operations and customer service matters. Typically, this is the department that will handle documentation, paperwork, and other service requests.

If you have selected a captive firm as the custodian for your retirement savings plan, you might be receiving your investment advice from a call center. Many large brokerage companies discourage their sales representatives from managing smaller accounts. In January 2012, Investment News reported in "Merrill Raises the Bar for its Brokers," that the account size minimums for one major brokerage house/bank were raised to $250,000. The sales reps who continued to service these smaller accounts had their commission severely reduced or completely eliminated for new business.[3]

Unfortunately, this is becoming a common trend in the captive brokerage industry. The consumer who is trying to do it on their own or is just simply building up a savings plan may find it more difficult to establish an ongoing advisory relationship with a call center. Of course, some investors may prefer this as their situation might not warrant a comprehensive plan/advisor.

Finally, you need to schedule specific dates to review your accounts with your advisor. Many clients prefer face-to-face meetings, but as long as you are comfortable with the arrangements for your situation just about any form of communication will suffice. You should anticipate communicating with your advisor regularly to review your plan and discuss any changes that may be needed.

Rule #10 – Succession plan for advisor

Another important question to ask your advisor is, "What happens to our money if you retire or pass away?"

It is quite ironic that many financial professionals help their clients to craft a plan for their future but haven't necessarily crafted one for themselves. You'll want to feel comfortable with the answer you receive to this question. Many professionals have multiple advisors in their office and/or have established a succession plan with somebody in the business that shares their same planning philosophies.

The details of how the transition will occur are important, and you need to fully understand how a change in advisors may impact your assets and your financial plan.

ENDNOTES

CHAPTER 1

1. William J. Wiatrowski, "The Last Private Industry Pension Plans: A Visual Essay," Bureau of Labor Statistics, Monthly Labor Review, December 2012, http://www.bls.gov/opub/mlr/2012/12/art1full.pdf
2. "The Underfunding of State and Local Pension Plans," Congressional Budget Office, May 4, 2011, https://www.cbo.gov/publication/22042
3. Olivia Mitchell, "Unfunded Pension Debts of U.S. States Still Exceed $3 Trillion," *Forbes*, August 25, 2015, https://web.stanford.edu/~rauh/research/UnfundedDebts.pdf
4. John Wasik, "Is Your Pension Plan Underfunded?" *Forbes*, September 3, 2014, http://www.forbes.com/sites/johnwasik/2014/09/03/is-your-pension-plan-underfunded/
5. Barbara A. Butrica, Howard M. Iams, Karen E. Smith, and Eric J. Toder, "The Disappearing Defined Benefit Pension and Its Potential Impact on the Retirement Incomes of Baby Boomers," Social Security Bulletin, Vol. 69, No. 3, 2009, http://www.ssa.gov/policy/docs/ssb/v69n3/v69n3p1.html
6. "States in Danger as Pension Underfunding of $4.7 Trillion Threatens Their Fiscal Health," Investor's Business Daily, November 19, 2014, http://www.investors.com/unfunded-pensions-for-public-unions-threaten-states-fiscal-health
7. Ibid.
8. Sophia Pearson and Terrence Dopp, "Christie Wins Court Battle Over Funding N.J. Pension Gap," Bloomberg, June 9, 2015, http://www.bloomberg.com/news/articles/2015-06-09/christie-wins-n-j-pension-court-battle-punts-funding-crisis-iapegdvt
9. *Pension Benefit Guaranty Corporation Annual Report Fiscal Year 2014*, Pension Benefit Guaranty Corporation, pages ii and 20, http://www.pbgc.gov/documents/2014-annual-report.pdf
10. *The National Debt & Federal Budget: 2016 Presidential Election Issue Guide*, FirstBudget.org, 2015, http://www.concordcoalition.org/publications/2015/0617/national-debt-and-federal-budget-2016-presidential-election-issue-guide
11. Research Note #3: Details of Ida May Fuller's Payroll Tax Contributions, Social Security Administration, Historian's Office, https://www.ssa.gov/history/idapayroll.html
12. Sheyna Steiner, "Will Social Security Be There When You Need It?" Bankrate, March 17, 2015, http://www.bankrate.com/finance/retirement/future-of-social-security.aspx
13. *The National Debt & Federal Budget: 2016 Presidential Election Issue Guide*, FirstBudget.org, 2015, http://www.concordcoalition.org/publications/2015/0617/national-debt-and-federal-budget-2016-presidential-election-issue-guide
14. Ibid.
15. Ibid.
16. Ibid.
17. Ibid.

CHAPTER 2

1. Sumit Agarwal, John C. Driscoll, Xavier Gabaix, and David Laibson, "The Age of Reason: Financial Decisions Over the Life-Cycle with Implications for Regulation," Social Science Research Network, October 19, 2009, http://ssrn.com/abstract=973790 or http://dx.doi.org/10.2139/ssrn.973790
2. Michael S. Finke, John S. Howe, and Sandra J. Huston, "Old Age and the Decline in Financial Literacy," Social Science Research Network, August 24, 2011, http://ssrn.com/abstract=1948627
3. Keith Jacks Gamble, Patricia A. Boyle, Lei Yu, and David A. Bennett, "How Does Aging Affect Financial Decision Making?" Center for Retirement Research at Boston College, January 2015, http://crr.bc.edu/briefs/how-does-aging-affect-financial-decision-making/

CHAPTER 5

1. Guide to Short-Term vs. Long-Term Capital Gains Taxes, TurboTax, https://turbotax.intuit.com/tax-tools/tax-tips/Investments-and-Taxes/Guide-to-Short-term-vs-Long-term-Capital-Gains-Taxes--Brokerage-Accounts--etc--/INF22384.html and Selina Maranjian, "Long-Term Capital Gains Tax Rates in 2016," The Motley Fool, May 5, 2016, http://www.fool.com/retirement/general/2015/12/14/long-term-capital-gains-tax-rates-in-2016.aspx
2. IRS, Retirement Topics – IRA Contribution Limits, December 23, 2015, https://www.irs.gov/retirement-plans/plan-participant-employee/retirement-topics-ira-contribution-limits
3. Ibid.
4. IRS, Taxable and Nontaxable Income, https://www.irs.gov/publications/p554/ch02.html and "Does an IRA Distribution Count as Income to Social Security?" The Motley Fool, http://www.fool.com/knowledge-center/does-an-ira-distribution-count-as-income-to-social.aspx
5. IRS, IRA FAQs – Distributions (Withdrawals), January 6, 2016, https://www.irs.gov/retirement-plans/retirement-plans-faqs-regarding-iras-distributions-withdrawals
6. IRS, Retirement Topics – Required Minimum Distributions (RMDs), January 6, 2016, https://www.irs.gov/retirement-plans/plan-participant-employee/retirement-topics-required-minimum-distributions-rmds
7. Ibid.
8. IRA, Retirement Plan and IRA Required Minimum Distributions FAQs, January 6, 2016, https://www.irs.gov/retirement-plans/retirement-plans-faqs-regarding-required-minimum-distributions
9. Ibid.
10. IRS, Rollovers of Retirement Plans and IRA Distributions, February 19, 2016, https://www.irs.gov/retirement-plans/plan-participant-employee/rollovers-of-retirement-plan-and-ira-distributions
11. Ibid.
12. IRS, IRA One-Rollover-Per-Year Rule, January 22, 2016, https://www.irs.gov/retirement-plans/ira-one-rollover-per-year-rule
13. IRS, IRS Clarifies Application of One-Per-Year Limit on IRA Rollovers, Allows Owners of Multiple IRAs a Fresh Start in 2015, October 9, 2015, https://www.irs.gov/uac/newsroom/irs-clarifies-application-of-one-per-year-limit-on-ira-rollovers-allows-owners-of-multiple-iras-a-fresh-start-in-2015

14. IRS, IRA One-Rollover-Per-Year Rule, January 22, 2016, https://www.irs.gov/retire-ment-plans/ira-one-rollover-per-year-rule
15. IRS, Traditional IRAs, https://www.irs.gov/publications/p590b/ch01.html
16. Ibid.

CHAPTER 6

1. IRS, Retirement Plan and IRA Required Minimum Distributions FAQs, January 6, 2016, https://www.irs.gov/retirement-plans/retirement-plans-faqs-regarding-required-minimum-distributions
2. IRS, Publication 590-A (2015), Contributions to Individual Retirement Arrangements (IRAs), https://www.irs.gov/publications/p590a/

CHAPTER 7

1. Rex Moore, "How Much Should You Really Count on Social Security for Your Retirement," The Motley Fool, August 30, 2014, http://www.fool.com/retirement/general/2014/08/30/how-much-should-you-really-count-on-social-securit.aspx
2. Mary Beth Franklin, "Social Security's Special Tax Rule for Repaying Benefits," Investment News, January 9, 2015, http://www.investmentnews.com/article/20150109/BLOG05/150109933/social-securitys-special-tax-rule-for-repaying-benefits
3. Social Security Administration, SSA Publication No. 05-10147, "When to Start Receiving Retirement Benefits," August 2015, https://www.ssa.gov/pubs/EN-05-10147.pdf
4. John Maxfield, "Retirement Planning: What Is the 4% Rule?" The Motley Fool, May 10, 2015, http://www.fool.com/retirement/general/2015/05/10/retirement-planning-the-4-percent-rule.aspx
5. Social Security Administration, SSA Publication No. 05-10035, "Retirement Benefits," https://www.ssa.gov/pubs/EN-05-10035.pdf, and SSA Publication No. 05-10072, "How You Earn Credits," January 2016, https://www.ssa.gov/pubs/EN-05-10072.pdf
6. Social Security Administration, SSA Publication No. 05-10072, "How You Earn Credits," January 2016, https://www.ssa.gov/pubs/EN-05-10072.pdf
7. Social Security Administration, "Retirement Planner: Can You Take Your Benefits Before Full Retirement Age?" https://www.ssa.gov/planners/retire/applying2.html
8. Social Security Administration, FAQs, "What is the Eligibility for Social Security Spouse's Benefits and My Own Retirement Benefits?" https://faq.ssa.gov/link/portal/34011/34019/Article/3754/What-is-the-eligibility-for-Social-Security-spouse-s-benefits-and-my-own-retirement-benefits
9. Social Security Retirement Planner, Benefits for You as a Spouse, https://www.ssa.gov/planners/retire/applying6.html
10. Ibid.
11. Social Security Retirement Planner, Benefits for Your Spouse, https://www.ssa.gov/planners/retire/yourspouse.html
12. Matthew Frankel, "3 Facts You Need to Know About Social Security Spousal Benefits," The Motley Fool, April 25, 2016, http://www.fool.com/retirement/general/2016/04/25/3-facts-you-need-to-know-about-social-security-spo.aspx
13. Social Security Retirement Planner, If You Are Divorced, https://www.ssa.gov/planners/

retire/divspouse.html

14. Social Security Retirement Planner, Benefits for Your Divorced Spouse, https://www.ssa.gov/planners/retire/yourdivspouse.html

15. Social Security Administration, "Benefit Amounts for the Surviving Spouse by Year of Birth," https://www.ssa.gov/planners/survivors/survivorchartred.html

16. Social Security Administration, SSA Publication No. 05-10069, "How Work Affects Your Benefits," January 2016, https://www.ssa.gov/pubs/EN-05-10069.pdf

17. Hallie Levine, "5 Reasons Women Live Longer Than Men," Health, October 13, 2014, http://news.health.com/2014/10/13/why-do-women-live-longer-than-men/

18. Maximize My Social Security, "Updates Based on Bipartisan Budget Act of 2015," 2016, https://maximizemysocialsecurity.com/updates-based-bipartisan-budget-act-2015

CHAPTER 8

1. Dalbar, April 9, 2014, http://www.dalbar.com/Portals/dalbar/cache/News/PressReleases/2014QAIBHighlightsPR.pdf

2. Ibid.

3. The Dubious Disciple, "Matthew 25:25, How Much Is a Talent?" October 17, 2011, http://www.dubiousdisciple.com/2011/10/matthew-2525-how-much-is-a-talent.html

CHAPTER 9

1. Crestmont Research, "Markowitz Misunderstood: MPT Should Come with a Warning Label," 2004, http://www.crestmontresearch.com/docs/Article-Markowitz.pdf

2. AQR Cliff's Perspective, "Efficient Frontier 'Theory' for the Long Run," December 10, 2014, https://www.aqr.com/cliffs-perspective/efficient-frontier-theory-for-the-long-run

3. Cathy Pareto, "Achieving Better Returns in Your Portfolio," Investopedia, February 15, 2005, http://www.investopedia.com/articles/05/021705.asp

4. Roger G. Ibbotson and Paul D. Kaplan, "Does Asset Allocation Policy Explain 40, 90 or 100 Percent of Performance?" *Financial Analysts Journal*, January-February 2000, Vol. 56, No. 1, CFA Institute.

5. Roger G. Ibbotson, "The Importance of Asset Allocation," *Financial Analysts Journal*, Vol. 66, No 2, CFA Institute, http://www.cfapubs.org/doi/pdf/10.2469/faj.v66.n2.4, and "Navigating Volatility by Combining Diverse Investment Approaches," Genworth Financial Wealth Management, August 2012, https://www.genworth.com/dam/Americas/US/PDFs/Consumer/corporate/GFWM_9060_NavVolClientWP_FLY_2012_07_C7403.pdf

6. Arun Muralidhar and Sanjay Muralidhar, "The Case for SMART Rebalancing," QFinance: The Ultimate Financial Resource, 4th edition

7. Stan McNeal, "For Major League Hitters, .280 Is the New .300," *USA Today*, August 29, 2014, http://www.usatoday.com/story/sports/mlb/2014/08/29/mlb-hitting-300/14801965/

8. Joe Boozell, "The List: Top 10 Shooters in the NBA," March 2, 2015, http://www.nba.com/2015/news/hca/03/02/the-list-top-10-shooter-in-the-nba/index.html

9. Eugene F. Fama and Kenneth R. French, "The Capital Asset Pricing Model: Theory and Evidence," *Journal of Economic Perspectives*, Vol. 18, Number 3, Summer 2004, http://www-personal.umich.edu/~kathrynd/JEP.FamaandFrench.pdf

10. Eugene F. Fama and Kenneth R. French, "A Five-Factor Asset Pricing Model," *National*

Bureau of Economic Research, September 2014, http://papers.ssrn.com/sol3/papers.cfm?abstract_id=2287202

11. AQR Cliff's Perspective, "Our Model Goes to Six and Saves Value From Redundancy Along the Way," December 17, 2014, https://www.aqr.com/cliffs-perspective/our-model-goes-to-six-and-saves-value-from-redundancy-along-the-way

CHAPTER 10

1. Sandra Kollen Ghizoni, "Nixon Ends Convertibility of US Dollars to Gold and Announces Wage/Price Controls," Federal Reserve History, August 1971, http://www.federalreservehistory.org/Events/DetailView/33

2. APMEX, Gold Prices Today Per Ounce & Gold Historical Chart, http://www.apmex.com/spotprices/gold-price

3. Aurelio Locsin, "Is Air Travel Safer Than Car Travel?" *USA Today*, 2008, http://traveltips.usatoday.com/air-travel-safer-car-travel-1581.html

4. Tim McMahon, "Average Annual Inflation Rates by Decade," June 18, 2015, http://inflationdata.com/Inflation/Inflation/DecadeInflation.asp

5. Lawrence Lewitinn, "Here's 222 Years of Interest Rate History on One Chart," Yahoo Finance, September 18, 2013, http://finance.yahoo.com/blogs/talking-numbers/222-years-interest-history-one-chart-173358843.html

6. Ibid.

7. Ibid.

CHAPTER 11

1. Ruth Helman, Greenwald & Associates; Craig Copeland, Ph.D.; and Jack VanDerhei, Ph.D., "The 2015 Retirement Confidence Survey: Having a Retirement Savings Plan a Key Factor in Americans' Retirement Confidence," Employee Benefit Research Institute, April 2015, https://www.ebri.org/pdf/briefspdf/ebri_ib_413_apr15_rcs-2015.pdf

2. Andrew Duggan, "Retirement Remains Americans' Top Financial Worry," Gallup, April 22, 2014, http://www.gallup.com/poll/168626/retirement-remains-americans-top-financial-worry.aspx

3. Allianz, "Retirement in America Will Never Be the Same," *Reclaiming the Future Study, 2010*, https://www.allianzlife.com/retirement-and-planning-tools/reclaiming-the-future/white-paper-findings

4. "Buy and Hold Strategy Explained," Money-Zine, December 2, 2015, http://www.money-zine.com/investing/investing/buy-and-hold-strategy-explained/

5. John Mauldin, "Economic Dithers as Eastern Europe Bad Debts to Bankrupting European Banks," The Market Oracle, February 21, 2009, http://www.marketoracle.co.uk/Article9018.html

6. William P. Bengen, "Determining Withdrawal Rates Using Historical Data," *Journal of Financial Planning*, October 1994, http://www.retailinvestor.org/pdf/Bengen1.pdf

7. Paul A. Merriman, "22 Things You Should Know About Bear Markets," *MarketWatch*, August 25, 2015, http://www.marketwatch.com/story/22-things-you-should-know-about-bear-markets-2015-08-05

8. Paul Merriman, "How Retirement Investors Hurt Themselves," MarketWatch, May 7, 2014, http://www.marketwatch.com/story/how-retirement-investors-hurt-

themselves-2014-05-07
9. Ibid.
10. Ibid.

CHAPTER 12

1. Family Caregiver Alliance, National Center on Caregiving, "Caregiver Health," 2006, https://www.caregiver.org/caregiver-health
2. Tricia O'Brien, "The Stress of Family Caregiving: Your Health May Be at Risk," Caregiver Action Network, Winter 2006, http://www.caregiveraction.org/_doc/pdf/CaregiverStress.pdf
3. Ibid.
4. Ibid.
5. Family Caregiver Alliance, National Center on Caregiving, "Caregiver Health," 2006, https://www.caregiver.org/caregiver-health
6. Blake Ellis, "Nursing Home Costs Top $80,000 a Year," CNN Money, April 9, 2013, http://money.cnn.com/2013/04/09/retirement/nursing-home-costs/index.html
7. American Association for Long-Term Care Insurance and Kiplinger, "Fresh Perspectives on Long-Term Care Planning Guide," http://www.aaltci.org/long-term-care-insurance-costs/
8. Genworth Financial 2016 Cost of Care Survey, "Compare Long Term Care Costs Across the United States," April 2016, https://www.genworth.com/about-us/industry-expertise/cost-of-care.html

CHAPTER 13

1. Art Kohn, "Brain Science: Focus – Can You Pay Attention?" *Learning Solutions Magazine*, June 12, 2014, http://www.learningsolutionsmag.com/articles/1440/brain-science-focuscan-you-pay-attention
2. Nina Porzucki, Public Radio International, March 7, 2014, http://www.pri.org/stories/2014-03-07/suzanne-massie-taught-president-ronald-reagan-important-russian-phrase-trust
3. Andrew Osterland, "Merrill Lynch Raises the Bar for Small Brokers," *Investment News*, January 8, 2012, http://www.investmentnews.com/article/20120108/REG/301089982/merrill-lynch-raises-the-bar-for-small-brokers

Andrew J. Paladino, CPA, MSF

Andrew ("Andy") J. Paladino is the founder and owner of Paladino Financial Group. Paladino Financial Group (PFG) is a comprehensive financial advisory firm that helps a variety of individuals, families, business owners, executives, professional athletes, and nonprofit organizations.

Andy is a presenter of various financial topics. He has also taught financial continuing education courses at area colleges and high schools. He is the host of a weekly local radio show, Your Financial Hour, heard on 105.7 FM, The Fan.

Andy works very closely with clients to fully understand their many challenges, goals and dreams. His clients can have confidence in knowing that Andy stays informed regarding important financial planning and industry developments through his involvement with various financial industry organizations.

He is a member of the American Institute of Certified Public Accountants (AICPA) and the Maryland Association of Certified Public Accountants (MACPA). Andy also actively participates in several nonprofit organizations, in activities at his children's school, and as a coach of local youth sports. He is currently Commissioner of Reisterstown Baseball and the middle school baseball coach at Park School. Additionally, Andy is involved and a coach in USA Hockey.

Andy graduated magna cum laude from Towson University with a Bachelor of Science in Business Administration, concentrating in Accounting and Finance. He then went on to obtain his Master of Science in Finance (MSF) from Loyola College. He has completed the Harvard Institute training program at Harvard University, an in-depth program of portfolio theory. Andy and his wife, Debbi, have fun staying active with their three children.

andyp@paladinofinancialgroup.com
www. paladinofinancialgroup.com

Andrew J. Paladino is an investment advisor representative of, and securities and advisory services are offered through, USA Financial Securities Corp. (Member FINRA/SIPC). USA Financial Securities is a registered investment advisor located at 6020 E. Fulton St., Ada, MI 49301. Paladino Financial Group is not affiliated with USA Financial Securities.

Craig J. Watkins, Managing Partner

Craig J. Watkins is the managing partner of Cornerstone Financial Group and has been in the insurance and financial industry since 1980, striving to provide the finest service and retirement advice to his clients. It doesn't matter how much money you have. His pure goal is to help others. He combines professional dedication and personal commitment to offer creative financial planning in the context of a personal, caring relationship. He believes that successful client relationships are built upon trust and personalized services. Craig provides comprehensive investment advice and regular communications.

Thorough and innovative, Craig demonstrates a seasoned understanding in meeting the needs of high net worth individuals, successful professionals, corporations, and business owners. He focuses on income distribution strategies and tax-advantaged asset accumulation and preservation strategies. Additionally, Craig's emphasis also includes investment asset allocation and designation, insurance protection, beneficiary planning, and qualified retirement plans.

He attended the University of California, Berkeley, on an athletic scholarship while studying business and accounting and is always continuing his career-related education studies. He is a member of the National Association of Insurance and Financial Advisors (NAIFA) and the Managing Partner of Cornerstone Financial Group in Walnut Creek, California.

In his leisure, Craig enjoys playing golf, riding his Harley Davidson, game hunting, fishing, and sports. He is happily married to Margaret, has raised three daughters, and resides in El Dorado, California.

www.cfgstrategies.com
craig@cfgstrategies.com

Craig Watkins is an investment advisor representative of, and securities and advisory services are offered through, USA Financial Securities Corp. (Member FINRA/SIPC). USA Financial Securities is a registered investment advisor located at 6020 E. Fulton St., Ada, MI 49301. Cornerstone Financial Group is not affiliated with USA Financial Securities. CA license #0591010

James V. Hartwell, CPA, CFP

James V. Hartwell is both a Certified Public Accountant and Certified Financial Planner™. He lives in Southwest Michigan where he has made his home with his wife and raised four children. Together they have enjoyed the ups and downs of running an accounting and wealth management business. Jim shares the journey of advising his clients with the wisdom and knowledge of his best friend and business partner Robert Wolf. Together they own and operate Hartwell & Wolf – Accountants and Wealth Management.

Jim has been in the financial services industry concentrating on the tax aspect of financial management since 1983. He is a graduate of Calvin College, located in Grand Rapids, Michigan. He opened his own CPA practice in 1989, and obtained his CFP designation in the same year. He was one of the first CPA's in West Michigan to hold both a CPA license and a CFP designation.

Jim obtained this CFP designation to bring all the aspects of planning to his client's life. Because of his comprehensive approach, Jim has relationships stretching back decades, and relationships that now include his clients' children. Clients have said that the firm of Hartwell & Wolf helps bring clarity to their financial life, simplifies the decision-making process, and offers them choices they didn't know existed.

Jim and Rob operate locations in St. Joseph and Kalamazoo, Michigan. They are still accepting clients as of the date of publication.

www.hartwellwolf.com

jhartwell@hartwellwolf.com

John Cindia, CFP, PFS

John Cindia of LifeStages Advisory works with closely held businesses, as well as affluent and high net worth individuals in the areas of tax, financial, wealth, insurance, and retirement planning.

John's breadth of experience has ranged from vice president of marketing for a Fortune 500 insurance company to running his own certified public accounting (CPA)/financial planning practice for affluent and high net worth clientele since 1984.

John's practice has always assisted clients with tax-efficient financial planning. In 1994, John became securities and insurance licensed to further assist clients with tax-advantaged retirement planning and tax-efficient investing for wealth accumulation purposes. Since 2000, investment management, retirement, and insurance planning has become a significant area of concern for aging boomers and John has adapted his concentration in these areas to accommodate client needs.

John graduated from the University of Akron in Akron, Ohio, with a bachelor's degree in accounting. In 1984, John became a licensed CPA in Ohio and later became licensed in the states of North Carolina and Florida as clients relocated. John studied to obtain the Personal Financial Specialist (PFS™) designation through the American Institute of CPAs (AICPA). John has also acquired the Series 6, 7, 24, 63 and 65 securities licenses; and life, health, disability, long-term care, and property/casualty licenses. He also has CPA affiliations with the American Institute of CPAs (AICPA), Florida Institute of CPAs (FICPA), North Carolina Association of CPAs (NCACPA) and Ohio Society of Certified Public Accountants (OSCPA), in addition to the Society of Financial Service Professionals.

LIFESTAGES ADVISORY
www.lifestagesadvisory.com
jcindia@lifestagesadvisory.com

John Cindia is an investment advisor representative of, and securities and advisory services are offered through, USA Financial Securities Corp. (Member FINRA/SIPC). USA Financial Securities is a registered investment advisor located at 6020 E. Fulton St., Ada, MI 49301. LifeStages Advisory is not affiliated with USA Financial Securities.

Earl Schultz, ChFC, CLU

A seasoned educator and public speaker, Earl Schultz is the founder and president of Strategic Wealth Advisory with offices in the Reading and Allentown areas of Pennsylvania. The company's motto "Retirement Strategies in an Uncertain World" resonates with the families in the communities it serves. Earl is passionate about helping clients always Plan First, Invest Second™.

Since opening the doors of his practice in 1994, Schultz has been using the latest and most creative planning strategies with clients. Understanding the importance of continuing education, Schultz has taken part in ongoing advisory training with nationally renowned IRA and retirement planning expert Ed Slott. Schultz's passion is teaching and implementing strategies that may allow his clients to potentially have more money for themselves now, more money in retirement, and eventually more money for their families.

Clients have frequently commented that one of Schultz's greatest strengths is his ability to take complex issues and break them down into simple concepts. As such, he has cherished the opportunity to teach adult continuing education classes within numerous school districts. Having taught more than 150 classes attended by thousands of individuals, Schultz has realized his goal of positively impacting the financial health of thousands of area residents through education.

Earl has the Chartered Financial Consultant (ChFC®) and Chartered Life Underwriter (CLU®) designations. He was born and raised in Allentown, Pa. He has resided close to Reading since 1977 with his wife, Debbie. Together they are proud of their two children, and their spouses, and five grandchildren.

www.strategicwealthadvisory.net
earl@strategicwealthadvisory.net

William "Bill" J. LaCasse, ChFC, RFC

When Bill began his investment career over 25 years ago in 1989, he realized that it wasn't what you earned, but what you kept after taxes that mattered. Bill's career focus thus became the study of income, gift and estate taxation, qualified plans law, and charitable planning tax law as it relates to investments. For the past 20 years, Bill has been giving educational seminars on investing, tax strategies, retirement plan distribution strategies and financial estate planning throughout the state of Missouri. He also is a recurring guest on a radio show every Wednesday at 8:40 a.m. on News/Talk 1150 AM KRMS and sponsors a financial radio show every Saturday from 8-9 a.m. on the same station.

In addition, Bill holds licenses to allow him to do business transactions in stocks, bonds, mutual funds, variable contracts, life insurance, health insurance, and to act as an investment advisor representative. He has completed The American College for financial planning Certified Financial Planner (CFP®) certification curriculum and holds the following designations: Chartered Financial Consultant (ChFC®) and Registered Financial Consultant (RFC®). He is also a member of the International Association of Registered Financial Consultants.

www.srgfinancialadvisors.com
bill@srgfinancialadvisors.com

Christopher Tanke

Christopher Tanke is the founder and president of Strategic Financial Group, an independent financial planning firm located in West Michigan. Chris is known for both his accumulation and distribution strategies for pre- and post-retirees, and his educational programs on retirement have been widely attended by residents throughout western Michigan.

As a retired Air Force Reserve Major/Chaplain, he brings valuable insight into family dynamics and their effect on legacy financial planning. Chris is a financial services professional whose securities licenses and qualifications include Investment Advisor Representative license, Series 65, along with licenses 6 and 63. Chris is also licensed in annuities, life and health insurance.

Chris resides in Grand Haven, Michigan, with his wife, Terri. He enjoys hunting, fishing, golf, reading and classical music.

STRATEGIC
FINANCIAL GROUP
Plan Smart, Retire Smart

www.strategicfg.net
ct@strategicfg.net

Donald W. Coplin CFP, CLU, ChFC

Don Coplin began his career as an agent in 1982 with The John Hancock. Since then, his career has evolved from being an insurance advisor to a manager of fee-based financial advisors to a partner in private practice. In December 2000, Don joined forces with his current business partner, Levi Edgecombe, to form Edgecombe & Coplin Wealth Strategies, LLC, thus enhancing the planning capabilities for their clients. His primary responsibility in the firm is the creation, monitoring and management of clients' investment accounts.

Don has a Certified Financial Planner (CFP®) designation and has the Chartered Financial Consultant (ChFC®) and Chartered Life Underwriter (CLU®) designations from The American College. He is a member of the National Association of Insurance and Financial Advisors and the Tacoma SW Chapter of the Society of Financial Service Professionals. Don has taught multiple classes for the Life Underwriters Training Council and is a member of their Fellowship.

Don and Levi were featured in *Proactive Advisor Magazine* as the cover story "Teamwork Multiplies Success" (March 17, 2016) and "The Power of Co-Op Radio Advertising" (April 14, 2016). He conducts monthly seminars on financial topics and is an occasional guest on the USA Financial Radio Show on Saturdays from 9-10 a.m., KLAY AM 1180 Talk Radio.

He and wife, Judy, married for more than 36 years, have two sons, Drew and Ben, and two grandsons. Although Don travels a lot, there's no better place than relaxing at home with Judy and the family's miniature schnauzer, Nina, and beagle, Olive, or playing the sax.

www.ecws4u.com
donc@ecws4u.com
levib@ecws4u.com

Levi B. Edgecombe CFP, CLU, ChFC

Levi B. Edgecombe began his career in 1971 with Equitable of Iowa following two years as a youth director at First Presbyterian Church in Tacoma, Washington. He has been involved in the financial services industry since that time. Levi and Don Coplin formed Edgecombe & Coplin Wealth Strategies, LLC in December 2000, so they could combine their strengths to better serve clients. Levi earned his Certified Financial Planner (CFP®) designation and has also received his Chartered Financial Consultant (ChFC®) and Chartered Life Underwriter (CLU®) designations from The American College. He's concentrated his professional development in the arenas of financial estate, business and retirement planning for both individuals and closely held companies.

Levi is the past president of the Tacoma SW chapter of the Society of Financial Service Professionals and is a member of the Tacoma Estate Planning Council. He has been the featured speaker several times for the Tacoma and Olympia Estate Planning Councils and has been a LUTCF instructor for Advanced Estate Planning. In 2008, Levi was a featured speaker at the Commonwealth Financial Network National Wealth Symposium.

Levi and Don were featured in *Proactive Advisor Magazine* as the cover story "Teamwork Multiplies Success" (March 17, 2016) and "The Power of Co-Op Radio Advertising" (April 14, 2016). He conducts monthly seminars on financial topics. He is a graduate of Wheaton College with a B.A. in Literature.

Levi and his wife, Denise, married in 1981 and have resided in Puyallup, Washington, since 1982 and have a son, Jesse, and daughter, Whitney. Levi has been involved with Young Life and has been an elder at Crossroads Covenant, his church for over 25 years.

EDGECOMBE & COPLIN
wealth strategies, LLC
Creative Wealth Management

www.ecws4u.com
donc@ecws4u.com
levib@ecws4u.com

Jim Yent, ChFC, and Teresa Yent, CLTC, ChFC

Jim and Teresa Yent are the owners of Golden Years Advisors, an independent financial services firm that focuses on retirement planning.

Teresa studied Business Administration at Lubbock Christian College. She has achieved numerous certifications and industry accolades including the Certified in Long-Term Care designation and Chartered Financial Consultant® (ChFC).

Jim graduated from Yale University where he was the captain of the basketball team, a member of Skull and Bones, and an a cappella singer in the Yale Whiffenpoofs. He spent over 20 years as a consultant to financial services firms such as Farmers Insurance, Credit Suisse First Boston, and Charles Schwab, to name a few. Jim is a Chartered Financial Consultant® (ChFC). He is also a 2017 Level III Candidate in the CFA Program.

Their professional practice, Golden Years Advisors LLC, caters exclusively to those aged 55 and above. Jim and Teresa's goal is always to do the right things at the right time for the right reasons for their clients' financial affairs.

Jim and Teresa are passionate advocates for retirees. They participate in Alzheimer fundraising, assist retirees in signing up for patient assistance drug programs, train retirees on how to use personal computers, and are active advocates for issues important to retirees and those close to retirement.

Golden Years Advisors

www.goldenyearsadvisors.com
teresa@goldenyearsadvisors.com
jim@goldenyearsadvisors.com

Drew Kellerman

A seasoned retirement planner and wealth advisor, Drew Kellerman is the founder of Phase 2 Financial LLC, an independent, fee-based financial planning company located in Gig Harbor, Washington.

Drew began his career in financial services during the late 1990s, following in the footsteps of his father and grandfather, both career investment professionals.

He provides a wide range of investment management and strategic wealth planning services for pre-retirees, retirees, and accomplished individuals.

Drew's goal is to serve as an unbiased advisor, guiding his clients on their quest for financial confidence. He works one-on-one with his clients to:
- develop balanced and innovative financial plans,
- implement those plans with the appropriate investments and financial tools,
- actively manage the plan and the investments, making adjustments when necessary.

Drew holds Life, Health and Long-Term Care insurance licenses, as well as securities license Series 65. The Series 65 exam, called The Uniform Investment Advisor Law Exam, covers laws, regulations, ethics and topics such as retirement planning, portfolio management strategies, and fiduciary responsibilities.

As a former Airborne Ranger infantry officer in the U.S. Army, Drew learned the value of developing detailed plans, executing complex strategies and readily adapting to changing and challenging environments. The plans he develops for his clients reflect and incorporate these experiences.

www.phase2financial.net
drew@phase2financial.net

Greg Zott

Greg Zott is president of GNZ Financial, an independent financial planning firm located in Troy, Michigan. GNZ Financial has provided financial services for both pre- and post-retirees since January 1988.

After completing his undergraduate degree in 1977 from the University of Michigan, Greg worked for the John Hancock Insurance company as an agent and then staff manager for 11 years. Those years were valuable in two ways:

1) learning the basic principles of financial planning, and,
2) finding out the limitations of a one-company advisor.

In January 1988, Greg started his own independent firm, GNZ Financial, out of his home. Greg was able to take what he learned from his experience with a big corporation and combine it with the benefits that an independent financial advisor can offer. The firm is currently celebrating 28 years in business.

Greg holds licenses for a variety of financial products and strategies and is also a licensed fiduciary. This approach assures clients that GNZ Financial acts first and foremost in the best interest of a client.

Greg is a member of the Financial Services Institute, Detroit Chamber of Commerce, and Better Business Bureau. He is married to his wife, Therese, for 39 years and has five sons. He currently resides in Birmingham, Michigan.

GNZ FINANCIAL
STRATEGIES & SOLUTIONS FOR THE 21ST CENTURY

www.gnzfinancial.com
greg@gnzfinancial.com

Barry S. Waronker, JD

Barry S. Waronker, JD is the Senior Partner and Chief Executive Officer of Informed Family Financial Services and has been dedicated to providing high-quality service to all of the firm's clients since it opened in January 2001.

A graduate of Temple University and The Golden Gate University School of Law, Barry's communication skills are on display in his company's many client bulletins, newsletters, seminars and informative workshops. Over the years, Barry has helped numerous families make difficult decisions, including how to manage the risk and cost of long-term care and disability. His professional knowledge and experience extend beyond traditional insurance solutions, including the use of creative planning tools to help meet the special challenges faced by clients and their aging loved ones. His professional licenses and designations include Series 6, 63, 65 and 7 securities industry registrations.

In a previous life, he was the head writer of the "Good Morning LA" TV Show, creator of the record album "The Firsta Family," and writer for numerous well-known entertainers. While a law student, he clerked for the US Attorney's office, was active as a volunteer Big Brother, and wrote and co-produced pro-bono a series of Emmy-winning TV commercials for Big Brothers and Sisters of San Francisco.

Away from the office, Barry is fond of crossword puzzles, billiards, golf at the Flourtown Country Club, and peddling along Forbidden Drive in the Wissahickon. He and his family are long-time residents of Blue Bell, Pa.

Informed Family
Financial Services

www.informedfamily.com
bwaronker@informedfamily.com

David Swanson, Sr.

David Swanson, Sr. is the founder and president of Swanson Financial Services, Inc. For over three decades, he has been helping clients with their retirement and financial planning needs.

David makes it his mission to further the financial education of others in the Pacific Northwest by conducting seminars and speaking at public engagements about retirement planning essentials.

David spent the first 10 years of his career as a representative at two major Wall Street investment firms. After determining that serving as an independent investment advisor would be in the best interests of his clients, he broke away from the investment firms and started his own company more consistent with his own philosophy and ideals. He has served on several not-for-profit boards such as Albertina Kerr Center for Children, Oregon Lacrosse Youth Association and was the Executive Vice President for the Portland State University athletic board.

David has keen interests in the outdoors and enjoys many activities such as fishing, tennis, golf and swimming. He is married with three children and a furry, four-legged "son" named Butch.

SWANSON FINANCIAL

www.swansonfinancial.com
advisor@swansonfinancial.com

David Swanson is an Investment Advisor Representative of Swanson Financial Services, Inc. A Registered Investment Advisor • 16016 Boones Ferry Road, Lake Oswego, OR 97035